the *perfectly*
roasted chicken

Mindy Fox

the *perfectly*
roasted chicken

Photography by Ellen Silverman

Kyle Books

dedication

To my parents, Neil and Phyllis, and my brother, Jason, with love;
your intuition, elegance, and exuberance at the stove have long
been an inspiration.

Kyle Books
Distributed by National Book Network
4501 Forbes Boulevard | Suite 200 | Lanham, MD 20706
(800) 462-6420

First published in 2010 in hardcover as *A Bird in the Oven and Then Some*

10 9 8 7 6 5 4 3 2 1

978-1-906868-99-4

Project Editor Anja Schmidt
Designer Carl Hodson
Photographer Ellen Silverman
Food Sylists Anne Disrude and Rebecca Jurkevich
Prop Stylists Bette Blau and Deborah Williams
Production Director Gemma John and Lisa Pinnell
Chickens by Murray's | www.murrayschicken.com | (800) 770-6347

Library of Congress Control Number: 2012955961

Color reproduction by Sang Choy
Printed and bound in China by C & C Offset Printing Co.

Contents

INTRODUCTION

Here is a love story about chicken. Or perhaps it's a chicken story about love. It begins in 2002 on a sultry summer night in the Deep South, when, chatting for hours around a hand-dug pit of slow-roasting pig, I fell for the affable gent who soon became my husband. It ends with the making of this book.

My sweet suitor was allergic to chicken; had been since he was a kid. A bit of a challenge, I thought. Still, it wasn't as if I had to keep kosher, go gluten-free, ditch all things dairy, or never crack a crustacean with my companion. As a freelance food writer and recipe developer, I couldn't altogether avoid preparing poultry at home, but save for a couple slipups, I kept Steve free from the discomfort that resulted from his eating both the bird and its broth.

Then the cravings came. Unaware at first, I soon perceived a pattern. Every time Steve traveled out of town, I'd fix a dinner of roast chicken then savor the surplus over my next few meals, tossing the tender pull-apart meat, crisp, salty-sweet skin, and rich natural juices into salads, soups, rice dishes, and more. If my beau returned home before I'd had a chance to finish the bird, he'd gaze at it longingly and try a taste to see if his sensitivity had dwindled. Sometimes it seemed as though it had, and then, well, maybe not.

Over a plate of pork buns, my then new editor and I discussed the unparalleled pleasures of simple home cooking. The idea for this book took shape. On the subway back uptown, excitedly dreaming up dishes, I sadly realized an irony: for the next four months I'd be roasting loads of birds, and poor Steve would enjoy nary a bite. My most valuable taster would be on an extended leave of absence.

Soon I was in the kitchen with a stack of raw chickens and a blank notebook and pen. I roasted the first bird. Bits of plump green olives, whole fennel seeds, fresh lemon zest, and chopped thyme mingled under the skin as it crisped. Unable to resist, Steve covered a juicy shred of the rested meat with a spoonful of warm jus, and popped it into his mouth. Standing at the counter, he continued to consume until nearly half of the bird was gone, without a hint of adverse reaction. Stunned and optimistic, we considered the best: the allergy had run its course. A few birds later, our hunch was confirmed. Steve had a new favorite dish, and I had my best critic back on my team. I couldn't have written this book without him.

Roasting chicken, like the cooking of most food, is very much about love. The simple dish is perfect for sharing and fairly certain to provide great happiness. One bird provides ample meat for a small group of friends or family. If you're eating solo, the leftovers make for delicious salads, sandwiches, and more (it is helpful to know, as you cook through this book, that a roasted 4-pound bird provides about 4 cups of shredded meat). And, for a party or larger crowd, or, if you want to ensure leftovers, two or more birds can be cooked side by side.

When I figured out how many delicious dishes I could make with roast chicken (ones that made good sense with the bird included, not just tossed in willy-nilly), I couldn't decide which was more exciting—roasting the bird, or using the cooked meat to make tasty pastas; hearty soups; sandwiches à la Cuba and Vietnam; salads made with crimson blood oranges and crisp fennel, or salty smoked almonds and fresh figs, and so on.

Try any roast chicken you make, one with Indian seasonings, say, or a Greek sort, or a convenient store-bought rotisserie bird, in many of the recipes in this book. Each bird will enhance the flavor of the other dishes a little differently and deliciously.

what makes a good bird, a good bird?

The best roast chicken you will ever make depends on three things: a good bird, good salt, and a little technical know-how. It's also helpful to have a few good simple tools. All are easy to procure or achieve.

"Good birds" include organic, grass-fed, heritage, antibiotic-free, certified humane, and properly raised local types, both from individual local farmers and family-farm brands, like Murray's, from Pennsylvania. (See Sources and Credits, page 170) The multitude of labels can be confusing but the following definitions, defined at the time of writing, will help. Try several good birds and see which you prefer.

GOOD BIRDS/LOOK FOR THESE ATTRIBUTES

Organic: Raised without antibiotics and fed only organic feed (free from synthetic fertilizers or pesticides).

Grass-fed or pasture-raised: Raised on a nutrient-rich, low-fat diet of fresh and, in the winter months, stored grasses. (See Sources and Credits, page 170.) Eating fresh grasses on their own schedules and spending much of their time outdoors greatly reduces the animals' need for antibiotics. Grass-fed meats are lean, yet rich in "good fat," including omega-3 fatty acids and conjugated linoleic acids (CLAs), both of which are helpful defenses against cancer. Feeding animals on grass also has environmental benefits: less fossil fuel is used to provide the diet; the animals naturally and organically fertilize the ground they graze on; the grazed pasture removes carbon dioxide from the atmosphere more effectively than any other land use; and more. Grass-fed birds can be cooked at the same temperature as their grain-fed counterparts, but may cook faster, since they are leaner. Use an instant-read thermometer and begin checking for doneness 10 to 15 minutes earlier than the stated recipe time. (For more information on grass-fed meat, see www.eatwild.com)

Raised without antibiotics: No antibiotics were used at any time during the raising of the bird, from pre-hatched eggs through processing. This does not mean, however, the bird is organic.

Local: Local can mean that the chicken was raised within a community, state, or region. The essence of the term is three-fold: the product traveled a shorter distance from farm to table than its commercially raised counterpart, thereby using minimal nonrenewable resources; purchasing the product supports the link between local farmer, consumer, economy, and the environment; and community is fostered between and among consumers and farmers. Local food is likely to be grown or raised responsibly. It may or may not be certified organic (many small farmers forgo official USDA certification, but often follow organic practices). Getting to know your farmer so you can discuss best practices is a terrific way to both understand how your food is being grown or raised, and to foster community.

Heritage breeds: Heritage refers to livestock breeds that were raised in the days before industrial agriculture caused a significant reduction in breed variety. These breeds are sustainably raised, which means raised with best practices for the animal, the community, and the environment. The meat of heritage breeds is firmer, juicier, and more flavorful than that of commercially raised animals, since the latter are bred not for flavor but to gain weight quickly and to withstand confined conditions. Heritage poultry breeds include Barred Plymouth Rock, Dark Cornish, and many more. Heritage breeds may require slightly different cooking times than commercial birds. Be sure to inquire when you buy. (For more information, see Sources and Credits, page 170, and www.sustainabletable.org.)

Kosher: Raised and slaughtered according to Jewish dietary rules. Because the birds are hand-salted during processing, the meat is saltier than non-kosher birds. Use less salt to season before cooking.

Certified humane: Living conditions for animals, from birth through slaughter, were above federal standards (see www.certifiedhumane.org for details).

Air-chilled: A system that uses cold air, as opposed to water, to chill chickens during processing. Air-chilled processing, the norm in Europe and Canada, is fairly new to the United States. Chilling is a necessary process; each method has its own benefits.

Retained water: Chickens that are not air-chilled during processing are chilled in water, some of which is retained, and the amount must be declared on the label.

BUYER BEWARE/THINGS TO AVOID

Enhanced: A solution of water, salt, and sodium phosphate is added to the bird to flavor and tenderize it. The solution can increase sodium levels to well over 400 milligrams per serving—nearly one-third the daily recommended amount for most people. The solution also increases the weight of the bird, and thereby the cost to the consumer. I recommend avoiding enhanced products and using good salt to season your meat instead.

Natural, free-range, and hormone-free: These three terms can be misleading. Food labeled "natural" does not contain any *artificial* ingredients, colorings, or chemical preservatives, and, in the case of meat and poultry, is minimally processed. However, meat from animals treated with artificial hormones, injected with saline solutions, or containing "natural flavors," such as processed proteins, can be dubbed "natural."

The label free-range, though it implies the bird had access to the outdoors and consumed grass as part of a varied diet, does not have to be verified.

Hormone-free, especially seen alone on a package for chicken, can be an empty claim, since federal regulations prohibit any commercial grower from adding hormones or steroids to chicken products. None of these terms mean that the bird was not fed antibiotics. Bottom line: look for more information and better product.

salts and peppers: key seasoning tools

I generally use flaky medium-coarse salts—the kind that crumbles easily in your fingertips (as opposed to larger and harder coarse salts, which are best for a grinding mill)—and fine sea salts for all of my cooking. Big Tree Farms makes a coarse "hollow pyramid" that is among my favorites

(see Sources and Credits, page 170). Sel gris, fleur de sel, and Maldon sea salt flakes and crystals are also terrific. Try various quality salts and see which you like best in both taste and texture.

For pepper, I purchase whole black peppercorns (buy them from a good purveyor to help ensure freshness), and I often tend to favor a very coarse grind, for the most distinctly peppery flavor. Most grinders don't do a coarse grind well, so I use the flat side of a chef's knife and a firm punch with the heel of my hand to smash the peppercorns into coarse pieces instead. Whole dried arbol chiles, Aleppo pepper (a sun-dried then ground red pepper grown in Syria and Turkey), and piment d'Espelette (a flavorful chile from France's Basque region) are complex peppers that can be used in place of, or in tandem with, black peppercorns (see Sources and Credits, page 170).

prepping the bird

Most of the recipes in this book call for whole birds, and there are some that require spatchcocked, or butterflied, birds, or whole birds cut into 10 pieces. Cutting up your own chicken is more economical than buying parts. You pay less per pound, and you also get more meat per pound, as precut meat is often poorly trimmed. There are many helpful visual resources on the Internet, should you need further help in spatchcocking or cutting up a whole bird.

To prep a whole bird: Remove the neck and giblets, then follow the recipe instructions, being sure to dry the bird well before seasoning (save the neck and backbone, if spatchcocking, to make broth; see page 100).

To spatchcock, or butterfly, a bird: Use a sharp pair of kitchen scissors to cut out the backbone by placing the chicken breast-side down, and cutting along one side of the backbone first, and then the other. Turn the bird breast-side up and gently but firmly press between the breasts to break the breastbone and flatten the bird, then tuck the wings under.

To cut a whole chicken into 10 pieces: With the chicken breast-side up, pull one leg away from the body. Use a sharp chef's knife to cut between the thigh and the body, removing the leg. Repeat with the other leg. Put one chicken leg, skin-side down, on the cutting board and, slicing firmly, cut the leg between the drumstick and the thigh. Repeat with the other leg. With the bird still breast-side up, remove the wings by slicing away the wing from the inside, just over the joint. Cut the carcass lengthwise into two halves—back portion and breast portion; cut the back portion crosswise into two pieces, then cut the breast lengthwise into two pieces.

roasting, resting, carving, and gravy or jus

I like to roast a bird until an instant-read thermometer registers 160°F in the breast, then let it rest for 10 to 20 minutes before carving (during which time the bird will cook a bit further).

To carve a roasted bird, put the bird on a cutting board, breast-side up, and cut off a leg by slicing the skin between the leg and the breast, then following the curve of the leg around the backside. Repeat with the other leg, then cut the drumsticks from the thighs. Cut the breast down the middle and serve it on the bone, or cut the wings from the body of the bird and then, cutting along each side of the breastbone, cut and use your hand to gently pull the breasts from the carcass. The breasts, off the bone, can be cut crosswise in half or into smaller pieces. Pull any delicious, tender meat from the bones and add them to your serving platter. There are two succulent pieces of meat lodged in the backbone, called the "oysters"—be sure to scoop these out with your fingers and eat them. The triangular tip at the base of the backbone (aka the butt bone) is scrumptious, too. The carcass will make a fantastic broth, and can be used right away or frozen for such purposes.

I am not fancy when it comes to making gravy or sauces for roasted birds. The pan juices created during roasting from the olive oil or butter, seasonings, and natural chicken fat are so divine on their own that I generally prefer to simply stir them up and spoon them over the cooked meat.

the best pans and a few basic kitchen tools for roasting your bird

My favorite pans for roasting chicken are an enameled cast-iron gratin (1½- to 3-quart pans are good sizes) and stainless-steel or cast-iron skillets (8- to 10-inch pans work well for a single bird). A small roasting pan is also good, though I prefer a pan with a lower edge to allow for more even heating on both the top and underside of the bird.

You don't need fancy tools to roast a great bird, just a few common ones:

An **oven thermometer** ensures that the temperature on the dial of your oven matches the one inside the appliance. Ovens often fall out of calibration, and, if you do not know that your appliance is running under or over the on-dial temperature, you are liable to under- or overcook your food.

A pair of **sharp kitchen scissors**, for spatchcocking, which is a fun term for butterflying. Joyce Chen is my favorite brand. (See page 9 for technique, and Sources for brand, page 170.)

A good **sharp chef's knife** (a "good knife" has a handle that fits comfortably in your hand and a high-quality blade).

A **cutting board**; **kitchen string** (tying the legs of a roast bird is not a must, but it looks nice); a **wooden spoon** and a wad of **paper towels** help to turn a bird during roasting, if the recipe requires. Use paper towels to dry the bird before seasoning.

An **instant-read thermometer** for testing doneness.

Good salt and pepper (see page 9).

the beauty of the freezer for roasted chicken, bones, and broths

While writing this book, I discovered a newfound love for my freezer. As I roasted chickens, I froze the necks, backs (when the chickens were butterflied), and, after the meat was eaten, the carcasses to use for delicious homemade broth. I froze the broth, as well as shreds of roast chicken, to use for future rice dishes, pastas, soups, stews, and more. Use resealable bags for chicken parts, carcasses, and shreds; airtight containers, leaving a 1-inch space at the top, for broth; and masking tape and a permanent marker to label and date items before freezing. It also helps to keep a list of what's in the freezer, to ensure items get used. I got everything I could from each and every bird, and it was all appreciated and enjoyed. Nothing was wasted. Using your freezer in this way is truly putting the "perfectly roasted chicken" philosophy to work.

Chapter one

ROASTING *the* BIRD

ROAST CHICKEN *with* BASIL, SCALLION, LEMON BUTTER, *and* POTATOES

Serves 4

I'll never tire of a butter-rubbed chicken roasted with rich, earthy potatoes tucked along its edges. Still, it's nice to update the classic pairing with a simple tweak or two. Here, when the bird is almost done, I sprinkle whole parsley leaves and squeeze a few lemon quarters over the potatoes, then pop the whole thing back into the oven. The herb leaves crisp up and the lemon pieces caramelize. Some might find the lemon rinds intense, but, if you like that sort of thing, you'll enjoy sliced bits of them with the rest of the dish.

1 (4-pound) whole chicken

1 cup thinly sliced fresh basil leaves

5 tablespoons unsalted butter, at room temperature

2 lemons

5 garlic cloves, thinly sliced

2 scallions, trimmed and thinly sliced

Flaky coarse sea salt

Freshly ground black pepper

1¾ pounds small to medium potatoes (about 1½ inches in diameter), cut lengthwise into quarters

2 tablespoons extra-virgin olive oil

1½ cups packed fresh flat-leaf parsley leaves, stems trimmed to 1 inch

Preheat the oven to 450°F with the rack in the middle. Pull off excess fat around the cavities of the chicken and discard, then rinse the chicken and pat dry very well, inside and out. From the edge of the cavity, slip a finger under the skin of each of the breasts, then gently but thoroughly loosen the skin from the meat of the breasts and thighs.

Put the basil and butter in a bowl. Finely zest the lemons into the bowl, holding the zester close so that you capture the flavorful oil that sprays from the lemons as you zest. Add the garlic and scallions and mix together to thoroughly combine.

Using your hands and working with about 1 tablespoon of the butter mixture at a time, gently push the mixture into the spaces you created between the chicken skin and meat, being careful not to tear the skin. As you work the mixture in, gently rub your hand over the outside of the skin to smooth out the mixture and push it farther down between the skin and meat where you may not be able to reach with your hand.

Season the chicken all over, using 2 to 3 teaspoons salt and generous pepper, then tie the legs together with kitchen string. In a large bowl, toss the potatoes with oil, ½ teaspoon salt, and generous pepper to coat well. Cut 1 lemon lengthwise into quarters and set aside.

Put a roasting pan (not nonstick) or 9x13-inch baking dish in the oven to heat for 10 minutes. Remove the pan from the oven and immediately put the potatoes and any oil left in the bowl into the pan, keeping them in as much of a single layer as possible, and push to the edges of the pan to make room for the chicken. Put the chicken into the pan, breast-side up. (It's fine if the bird sits on some of the potatoes.)

your pick of potatoes

My favorite potatoes to use for this dish are a mix of farmers' market varieties, including fingerlings, Adirondack Reds and Blues, yellow Carolas, and more. It's fine to purchase potatoes of different shapes and sizes, just be sure to cut them into roughly same-size pieces so that they cook through at the same rate.

Roast for 20 minutes, then remove the pan from the oven and turn the chicken breast-side down. Continue to roast for another 20 minutes, then remove the pan from the oven and turn the bird breast-side up again. Sprinkle the parsley over the potatoes then stir the parsley and potatoes to coat with the pan drippings. Squeeze 3 lemon quarters over the chicken, and put the squeezed rinds into the roasting pan. Continue to roast until the juices of the chicken run clear when the thigh is pierced with a fork, 20 to 30 minutes more.

Remove from the oven and let the chicken rest in the pan for 15 minutes, then transfer to a cutting board. Let rest for another 5 minutes, then carve. Spoon the pan juices over the chicken and serve with the potatoes and roasted lemons.

ROAST CHICKEN *with* GREEN OLIVES, FENNEL SEEDS, *and* THYME

Serves 4

If an olive can "make" a roast chicken, then this is the bird that proves it. Mild and fruity, there are two types of olives that work well in this dish, blending with the floral flavors of fennel seed and thyme: France's prized Lucques (originally Italian, but now mainly cultivated in the Languedoc), and the Cerignola, from Apulia, Italy. Both are large, meaty, deliciously fruity sorts, with barely a hint of salt.

1 (4-pound) whole chicken

1 cup green olives, preferably Lucques or Cerignola (about 10), pitted

2½ tablespoons fresh thyme leaves

1 garlic clove

2 lemons

1¾ teaspoons fennel seeds

½ tablespoon flaky coarse sea salt, plus more for serving

---

two ways to pit

To pit olives, use the side of a chef's knife, with the base of your palm on top, to press down on one olive at a time. Some pits will pop out of the flesh effortlessly. If they hold tight, use a sharp paring knife to cut the flesh away.

Preheat the oven to 425°F with the rack in the middle.

Pull off excess fat around the cavities of the chicken and discard, then rinse the chicken and pat dry very well, inside and out. From the edge of the cavity, slip a finger under the skin of each of the breasts, then use your fingers to gently but thoroughly loosen the skin from the meat of the breasts and thighs.

Mound the olives, thyme, and garlic on your cutting board and chop them up together, then zest the lemons over the olive mixture, holding the zester close to the mixture so that you capture the flavorful oil that sprays from the lemons as you zest. Chop the mixture together a little more, then mix in the fennel seeds.

Using your hands and working with about 1 tablespoon of the olive mixture at a time, gently push the mixture into the spaces you created between the chicken skin and meat, being careful not to tear the skin. As you work the mixture in, gently rub your hand over the outside of the skin to smooth out the mixture and push it farther down between the skin and meat where you may not be able to reach with your hand.

Tie the legs together with kitchen string and put the chicken into a baking dish or skillet a bit larger than the chicken and season with the salt. Roast in the oven, turning the pan once, halfway through, until the juices run clear when a thigh is pierced with a fork, about 1 hour to 1 hour and 15 minutes. Remove the pan from the oven and let the chicken rest in the pan for 15 minutes, then baste with the juices.

Transfer the chicken to a cutting board and let rest for 5 minutes, then carve and serve with the pan juices and extra salt for sprinkling.

SEA SALT ROAST CHICKEN
with DELECTABLY CRISPY SKIN

Serves 4

Mixing up tasty butters, brines, and rubs for roasted birds is a wonderful pursuit that rewards with tasty results. But there are times when the ease of a simpler recipe can't be beat. Enter this no-fuss, crispy-skinned bird. The recipe is more technique-focused than ingredient-driven. No oil or butter is used. The skin crisps in its own fat, with the aid of the salt, which provides flavor and reduces moisture. The key is to dry the bird very well before roasting; some like to air-dry the bird, loosely covered or uncovered, on a rack overnight in the refrigerator. But I find you can get a nice crispy skin without the overnight drying technique, as long as the bird is thoroughly dried with paper towels before it goes into the oven.

1 (4-pound) whole chicken

4 short leafy fresh herb sprigs (rosemary, thyme, and/or marjoram), optional

Flaky coarse sea salt

Freshly ground black pepper

Preheat the oven to 425°F with the rack in the middle. Pull off excess fat around the cavities of the chicken and discard, then rinse the chicken and pat dry very well, inside and out. From the edge of the cavity, slip a finger under the skin of each of the breasts, then gently but thoroughly loosen the skin from the meat of the breasts and thighs. Tuck the herb sprigs into the spaces you created, being careful not to tear the skin. Tie the legs together with kitchen string. Season the chicken all over, using 2 heaping tablespoons of coarse salt and generous pepper.

Heat a 9- to 10-inch cast-iron or ovenproof skillet, or a 1½- to 3-quart enameled cast-iron gratin in the oven for 15 minutes then remove the hot skillet from the oven and immediately put the chicken in the pan, breast-side up and put the pan back into the oven (remember, the handle is hot).

Roast for 15 minutes, then reduce the heat to 350°F and continue to roast, turning the pan once halfway through, until the juices of the chicken run clear when the thigh is pierced with a fork, 1 hour to 1 hour and 15 minutes more.

Remove the bird from the oven, sprinkle with a little more salt and let rest for 10 minutes, then transfer to a serving plate or cutting board. Spoon and discard the clear fat from the pan, leaving the drippings behind. Spoon the pan drippings and juices over the bird to serve.

ROAST CHICKEN *with* MUSTARD BUTTER

Dijon mustard and a good slab of butter are staples in my fridge. Here, they work together nicely to flavor this simple bird. A simple sauté of mustard greens or other greens, and Scalloped Potatoes with Goat Gouda and Thyme (page 49) make nice sides.

Serves 4

1 (4-pound) whole chicken

4 tablespoons unsalted butter, at room temperature

2 tablespoons finely chopped shallot

2 tablespoons Dijon mustard

2 tablespoons finely chopped fresh sage leaves

1 lemon

Flaky coarse sea salt

Freshly ground black pepper

Preheat the oven to 450°F with the rack in the middle. Pull off excess fat around the cavities of the chicken and discard, then rinse the chicken and pat dry very well, inside and out. From the edge of the cavity, slip a finger under the skin of each of the breasts, then gently but thoroughly loosen the skin from the meat of the breasts and thighs.

Put the butter, shallot, mustard, and sage in a bowl. Finely zest the lemon into the bowl, holding the zester close so that you capture the flavorful oil that sprays from the lemon as you zest. Mix all the ingredients together to thoroughly combine.

Using your hands and working with about 1 tablespoon of the butter mixture at a time, gently push the mixture into the spaces you created between the chicken skin and meat, being careful not to tear the skin. As you work the mixture in, gently rub your hand over the outside of the skin to smooth out the mixture and push it farther down between the skin and meat where you may not be able to reach with your hand.

Cut the lemon into quarters and stuff the pieces into the cavity of the bird. Tie the legs together with kitchen string. Season the chicken all over, using 2 to 3 teaspoons salt and generous pepper.

Put a roasting pan (not nonstick) or 9x13-inch baking dish in the oven to heat for 10 minutes. Remove the pan from the oven and immediately put the chicken into the pan, breast-side up. Roast for 35 minutes, then rotate the pan and reduce the heat to 375°F. Continue roasting, basting with the juices occasionally, until the juices run clear when a thigh is pierced with a fork, 25 to 35 minutes more. Remove the chicken from the oven and let it rest in the pan for 15 minutes, then baste with the juices.

Transfer the chicken to a cutting board and let rest for 5 minutes, then carve and serve with the pan juices and extra salt for sprinkling.

DEVIL'S CHICKEN *with* SWEET PEPPERS *and* ONIONS (ROAST CHICKEN DIAVOLO)

Diavolo means "devil" in Italian, which speaks to the peppery character of this tasty bird. The roasted peppers and onion provide a sweet counterbalance to the spice. Preparing the chicken in "spatchcock" style (removing the backbone and then slightly flattening the bird) makes for quick cooking and easy carving, and offers a nice change of pace from a whole bird.

Serves 4

1 (4-pound) whole chicken, backbone removed, breastbone cracked, and legs slashed through the flesh in 3 places (see page 9)

2 tablespoons plus 1 teaspoon extra-virgin olive oil, plus more for greasing

1 lemon

2 tablespoons finely chopped fresh rosemary, marjoram, and/or oregano leaves

1 tablespoon freshly ground black pepper

2 crumbled whole dried arbol chiles or ¾ teaspoon red pepper flakes

Flaky coarse sea salt

2 red bell peppers, cut into ½-inch strips

1 large yellow onion, peeled, cut lengthwise into ½-inch wedges, keeping ends intact

½ cup dry white wine

Preheat the oven to 425°F with the racks positioned in the middle and upper third of the oven. Line a baking sheet with parchment paper.

Pull off excess fat around the cavities of the chicken and discard, then rinse the chicken and pat dry very well, inside and out. Lightly grease a 12-inch heavy ovenproof skillet (not nonstick) or large baking dish with oil. Place the chicken, skin-side up, into the pan.

Finely zest the lemon into a small bowl, holding the zester close so that you capture the flavorful oil that sprays from the lemon as you zest. Stir together the lemon zest and 1 tablespoon juice, herbs, black pepper, and chiles. Spread the mixture all over the chicken, and under the skin of the breasts. Season generously with salt and drizzle with the 1 teaspoon oil.

Place the bell peppers and onion onto the prepared baking sheet and drizzle with the remaining 2 tablespoons oil. Using your hands, gently toss the vegetables to coat with oil, then arrange in a single layer. Season with salt and black pepper.

Roast the chicken on the upper rack and the vegetables on the middle rack for 20 minutes. Add the wine to the pan with the chicken and continue roasting for 10 minutes more. Remove both pans from the oven and, using a spatula or tongs, transfer the peppers and onions to the pan with the chicken, arranging the vegetables around the bird. Return the chicken to the oven and continue roasting until the skin is golden and the chicken is cooked through, 20 to 25 minutes more.

Remove from the oven and let rest 10 to 15 minutes, then transfer the chicken to a cutting board and let rest for 5 minutes more before carving. Serve with the peppers and onions, and the juices spooned over the top.

ROAST CHICKEN *in* PORCHETTATA

Serves 4

My friend, chef Sara Jenkins, inspires me in all things *porchetta*—a fabulously aromatic, succulent, slow-roasted pig stuffed with a heady mixture of herbs and garlic—and so was the inspiration for this bird. At Sara's eponymous New York City shop, you can purchase her pork by the sandwich or plateful. In Italian, "Porchettata" means "in the style of porchetta." No, chicken is not pork. But this bird does right—!—by its namesake cousin.

1 (4-pound) whole chicken

4 tablespoons unsalted butter, at room temperature

3 garlic cloves, finely chopped

1½ tablespoons finely chopped fresh sage leaves

1 tablespoon wild fennel pollen (see Sources and Credits, page 170)

1 tablespoon finely chopped fresh rosemary leaves

1 tablespoon finely chopped fresh thyme leaves

Flaky coarse sea salt

Freshly ground black pepper

Preheat the oven to 450°F with the rack in the middle. Pull off excess fat around the cavities of the chicken and discard, then rinse the chicken and pat dry very well, inside and out. From the edge of the cavity, slip a finger under the skin of each of the breasts, then gently but thoroughly loosen the skin from the meat of the breasts and thighs.

In a bowl, mix together the butter, garlic, sage, fennel pollen, rosemary, and thyme.

Using your hands and working with about 1 tablespoon of the butter mixture at a time, gently push the mixture into the spaces you created between the chicken skin and meat, being careful not to tear the skin. As you work the mixture in, gently rub your hand over the outside of the skin to smooth out the mixture and push it farther down between the skin and meat where you may not be able to reach with your hand. Tie together the legs with kitchen string. Season the chicken all over, using 1 tablespoon coarse salt and generous pepper.

Put a roasting pan (not nonstick) or 9x13-inch baking dish in the oven to heat for 10 minutes. Remove the pan from the oven and immediately put the chicken into the pan, breast-side up. Roast for 35 minutes, then rotate the pan and reduce the heat to 375°F. Continue roasting, basting with the juices occasionally, until the juices run clear when a thigh is pierced with a fork, 25 to 35 minutes more. Remove the bird from the oven and let it rest in the pan for 15 minutes, then baste with the juices.

Transfer the chicken to a cutting board and let rest for 5 minutes, then carve and serve with the pan juices and extra salt for sprinkling.

MOORISH-*style* ROAST CHICKEN

Serves 4

Sometimes all it takes is a simple rounding up of basic pantry spices to give a bird a subtle yet complex flavor. In this case cumin, coriander, and turmeric are blended with the lesser-known, yet increasingly popular, rich, smoky flavors of Pimentón de la Vera (Spanish smoked paprika). Pimentón de la Vera varies from sweet, "dulce," to bittersweet and slightly spicy, "agridulce," and spicy, "picante," any one of which work well in this recipe.

1 (4-pound) whole chicken

3½ tablespoons unsalted butter, at room temperature

¾ teaspoon ground cumin

½ teaspoon Pimentón de la Vera (see Sources and Credits, page 170)

¼ teaspoon turmeric

¼ teaspoon ground coriander

Flaky coarse sea salt

Freshly ground black pepper

Preheat the oven to 425°F with the rack in the middle. Pull off excess fat around the cavities of the chicken and discard, then rinse the chicken and pat dry very well, inside and out. From the edge of the cavity, slip a finger under the skin of each of the breasts, then gently but thoroughly loosen the skin from the meat of the breasts and thighs.

In a bowl, mix together the butter, cumin, Pimentón de la Vera, turmeric, and coriander.

Using your hands and working with about 1 tablespoon of the butter mixture at a time, gently push the mixture into the spaces you created between the chicken skin and meat, being careful not to tear the skin. As you work the mixture in, gently rub your hand over the outside of the skin to smooth out the mixture and push it farther down between the skin and meat where you may not be able to reach with your hand. Tie the legs together with kitchen string. Season the chicken all over, using 1 tablespoon salt and generous pepper.

Put a roasting pan (not nonstick) or 9x13-inch baking dish in the oven to heat for 10 minutes. Remove the pan from the oven and immediately put the chicken into the pan, breast-side up. Roast for 15 minutes, then rotate the pan and reduce the heat to 350°F. Continue roasting, basting with the juices occasionally, until the juices run clear when the thigh is pierced with a fork, about 1 hour more. Remove the chicken from the oven and let it rest in the pan for 15 minutes, then baste with the juices.

Transfer the chicken to a cutting board and let rest for 5 minutes, then carve and serve with the pan juices and extra salt for sprinkling.

GREEK ROAST CHICKEN *with* CAPER BUTTER, ROAST LEMONS, *and* SKORDALIA

Serves 4

Mmmmmm. Anything Greek is delectable to me, and especially with *skordalia*, the thick, somewhat tangy, garlic-heavy mash of potatoes (and sometimes nuts or bread) that is served as a condiment for meats, a spread for warm pita bread, and more. If you're not a garlic fan, you can make this chicken without its pungent accompaniment, and be quite happy. Bites of the roasted, somewhat caramelized lemons can be eaten with the chicken and *skordalia*, rind and all. While their flavor is intense, those who like it will enjoy.

1 (4-pound) whole chicken

3 tablespoons capers, preferably salt-packed, rinsed, soaked in cold water for 10 minutes, then rinsed again

5 tablespoons unsalted butter, at room temperature

2 lemons

1 tablespoon dried oregano, preferably Greek (see Sources and Credits, page 170)

Flaky coarse sea salt

Freshly ground black pepper

Pita bread for serving

SKORDALIA

½ pound Yukon gold potatoes

3 garlic cloves, finely chopped

¼ teaspoon fine sea salt

⅛ teaspoon freshly ground black pepper

2 tablespoons red wine vinegar

6 tablespoons extra-virgin olive oil

Preheat the oven to 450°F with the rack in the middle.

To make the *skordalia*: Peel the potatoes and cut them into 1-inch cubes. Combine with 5 cups cold water in a 3-quart heavy saucepan, then bring to a boil. Reduce heat and simmer, partially covered, until tender, 10 to 12 minutes. Drain in a colander and let cool to room temperature. Push through a potato ricer or gently mash with a fork.

Meanwhile, prepare the chicken: Pull off excess fat around the cavities of the chicken and discard, then rinse the chicken and pat dry very well, inside and out. From the edge of the cavity, slip a finger under the skin of each of the breasts, then gently but thoroughly loosen the skin from the meat of the breasts and thighs.

Pat the capers dry, then roughly chop and put them in a bowl with the butter. Finely zest the lemons into the bowl, holding the zester close so that you capture the flavorful oil that sprays from the lemons as you zest. Add the oregano then mix to thoroughly combine. Cut 1 lemon lengthwise into quarters and set aside.

Using your hands and working with about 1 tablespoon of the butter mixture at a time, gently push the mixture into the spaces you created between the chicken skin and meat, being careful not to tear the skin. As you work the mixture in, gently rub your hand over the outside of the skin to smooth out the mixture and push it farther down between the skin and meat where you may not be able to reach with your hand. Tie the legs together with kitchen string. Season the chicken all over, using 2 to 3 teaspoons salt and generous pepper. Put a roasting

pan (not nonstick) or 9x13-inch baking dish in the oven to heat for 10 minutes. Remove and immediately place the chicken inside, breast-side up. Roast for 20 minutes, then turn breast-side down. After 10 minutes, squeeze half of the juice from each lemon quarter over the chicken, and drop the quarters into the pan. Continue to roast until the juices of the chicken run clear when the thigh is pierced with a fork, 20 to 30 minutes more.

Remove from the oven and let rest for 5 minutes. Meanwhile return to the *skordalia*: Use the side of your knife and the blade to alternately chop and gently scrape the garlic and salt together, until you have a garlic paste. Transfer to a large wooden bowl. Add the potatoes and pepper. Using a large wooden spoon, pound and stir the mixture together just to combine. Add the vinegar in a slow but steady stream, while still pounding, until incorporated. Repeat with the oil. Transfer to a serving bowl.

Carve the chicken on a cutting board. Serve with the pan juices, *skordalia*, lemons, and pita.

Note: *Skordalia* can be made up to 3 hours ahead and kept in a sealed container in the refrigerator until ready to serve. If the oil separates, stir together before serving.

---

seek out salt-packed

When you have a choice, go for salt-packed capers over those jarred in vinegar. Salted capers are plumper, meatier in texture, and livelier in flavor than those brined in vinegar, which have a tinny, acidic taste that detracts from the main attraction.

POT-ROASTED CHICKEN *with* SLAB BACON, CELERY ROOT, *and* ROSEMARY

Serves 4

A heavy Dutch oven. Piney rosemary. Sweet celery root. Salty-rich slab bacon. Crushed juniper berries. Homemade broth. Calvados. A good chicken. This is my winter roast chicken mantra. Say it to yourself a few times, make it once or twice, and it might become yours as well. Use a high-quality bird (see page 6); those with a solution added for flavor not only taste inferior, they dilute this bird's delicious juices.

1 (4-pound) whole chicken

5 slices slab or thick-cut bacon, cut crosswise into 1-inch pieces

1½ pounds celery root, peeled and cut into 1½- to 2-inch chunks (see Box)

Flaky coarse sea salt

Freshly ground black pepper

½ cup Calvados

1 tablespoon fresh rosemary leaves

½ teaspoon whole juniper berries, coarsely chopped

---

wrangling the root

Celery root is very simple to cut: Slice off the top and bottom first, then, using a knife or vegetable peeler, cut away the skin and roots. Small, heavy roots offer a denser, more tender flesh than larger, lighter ones, which may have hollow spots inside. Be sure to cut celery root to the size indicated; smaller pieces get mushy and larger ones won't cook through.

Preheat the oven to 375°F with the rack in the middle. Pull off excess fat around the cavities of the chicken and discard, then rinse the chicken and pat dry very well, inside and out. Tie the legs together with kitchen string.

Heat a 5½- to 7-quart Dutch oven over medium heat. Add the bacon and cook, stirring occasionally, until it releases some fat and begins to brown, 3 to 4 minutes, then add the celery root and cook, stirring, until just lightly golden, about 5 minutes more. Remove the bacon and celery root from the pot, leaving the pot on medium heat.

Season the chicken all over with about 1 tablespoon coarse salt and generous pepper, then put the chicken, breast-side down, into the pot; reduce the heat to medium-low and cook, undisturbed, until the breast is lightly golden, about 5 minutes.

Turn the chicken breast-side up, increase the heat to medium-high, and cook for 1 minute. Add the Calvados and let it come to a boil, then carefully ignite with a kitchen match, keeping the lid of the pot nearby to extinguish the flames, if necessary. When the flames die out, add ½ cup water to the pot. Return the bacon and celery root to the pot and sprinkle the top of the bird with the rosemary and juniper. Seal the pot with foil, then fit the lid on well.

Roast the bird in the oven for 1 hour, then remove the pot, uncover, and let the bird rest for 15 minutes. Transfer to a cutting board, let rest for 5 minutes, then carve and serve with the celery root, bacon, pan juices, and salt for passing around the table.

SALAMI-BARDED, SALT-ROASTED CHICKEN *with* FENNEL SLAW

Roasting a whole chicken in a thick salt crust results in delectably tender meat that falls off the bone. The salt forms a barrier between the bird and the dry heat of the oven, then, in chunks, simply lifts off the bird after it is cooked. Barding in salami lends an added meaty flavor.

Serves 4

CHICKEN

1 (4-pound) whole chicken

4 garlic cloves, thinly sliced

1 tablespoon fresh thyme leaves

5 large egg whites

7¼ cups kosher salt (about 2 pounds)

4½ ounces thinly sliced salami

FENNEL SLAW

2 medium fennel bulbs, thinly sliced

4 tablespoons good-quality extra-virgin olive oil

3 tablespoons fresh lemon juice

3 tablespoons finely chopped fresh chives

Flaky coarse sea salt

Freshly ground black pepper

Preheat the oven to 400°F with the rack in the middle. Line a 9x13-inch baking dish with foil, leaving 2 to 3 inches on the long sides.

Pull off excess fat around the cavities of the chicken and discard, then rinse the chicken and pat dry very well, inside and out. From the edge of the cavity, slip a finger under the skin of each of the breasts, then gently but thoroughly loosen the skin from the meat of the breasts and thighs.

Finely chop together the garlic and thyme. Using your hands, gently push about two-thirds of the thyme mixture into the spaces between the chicken skin and meat, being careful not to tear the skin. As you work the mixture in, gently rub your hand over the outside of the skin to smooth out the mixture and push it farther down between the skin and meat where you may not have been able to reach with your hand. Rub the remaining garlic and thyme over the skin on the breast of the bird. Tie the legs together with kitchen string.

In a large bowl, whisk the egg whites until frothy. Add the kosher salt and stir to combine. Put 2 cups of the salt mixture into the prepared baking dish and press it into a flat bed for the chicken.

Layer about two-thirds of the salami, overlapping the pieces, over the breasts and sides of the bird, then gently press to adhere. Place the bird on top of the salt, breast-side down, then layer the remaining salami on top. Use the remaining salt mixture to form a complete shell around the chicken. Roast for 2 hours, turning the pan once halfway through.

When the chicken is about 30 minutes from being done, make the fennel slaw: Put the fennel, oil, and lemon juice in a large bowl; toss to combine. Add the chives and toss once more. Season with salt and pepper.

When the chicken is done, transfer the pan to a wire rack and let rest for 10 minutes, then break the salt crust and remove it (be careful as the steam may be hot; it is fine to let the bird cool further, if necessary).

Transfer the chicken to a cutting board. Pull off and discard any remaining salami. Carve and serve with the fennel slaw.

ROAST CHICKEN *with* MORCILLA SAUSAGE *and* PIMENTÓN DE LA VERA

Serves 4

Our friends Angelica and Marcos Intriago own Despaña, a fabulous shop in New York City's Soho, where we purchase all sorts of Spanish foodstuffs. Their homemade morcilla, a rich blood sausage flavored with onions and sweet spices, inspired this recipe. On chilly fall or winter nights, we enjoy this dish hot out of the oven, paired with Pomme Frites with 3 Mayos (page 50). In summer, we tote it to the park with cold Green Rice (page 52), a loaf of rustic bread, a hunk of tangy Mahon cheese, and a chilled red or white Rioja.

1 (4-pound) whole chicken, backbone removed, breastbone cracked (see page 9)

1½ teaspoons extra-virgin olive oil, plus more for greasing

2 garlic cloves, thinly sliced

1 tablespoon fresh rosemary leaves

1 teaspoon Pimentón de la Vera (see Sources and Credits, page 170)

14 ounces morcilla sausage (see Sources and Credits, page 170)

Flaky coarse sea salt

Freshly ground black pepper

1 cup dry red wine

Preheat the oven to 425°F with the rack in the middle. Lightly grease a 9x13-inch baking dish with oil.

Pull off excess fat around the cavities of the chicken and discard, then rinse the chicken and pat dry very well, inside and out. Put the chicken, skin-side up, into the baking dish.

Finely chop together the garlic and rosemary, then put the mixture into a small bowl. Add the Pimentón de la Vera and ½ teaspoon of the oil; stir to combine. Spread two-thirds of the mixture under the skin of the breasts and thighs; spread the remaining third over the skin of the breasts. Thinly slice about 1 ounce of the sausage. Push the slices under the skin of the breasts and thighs. Season the chicken all over, with 2 to 3 teaspoons of salt and generous pepper. Drizzle with the remaining 1 teaspoon oil.

Roast the chicken for 20 minutes. Meanwhile, slice the remaining sausage links in half crosswise on the diagonal.

Remove the bird from the oven, pour the wine over it, and add the sausages to the baking dish. Continue roasting, basting the bird and sausages with the pan juices occasionally, until the juices of the chicken run clear when the thigh is pierced with a fork, 30 to 35 minutes more.

Remove from the oven and let the chicken rest for 5 minutes, then transfer the bird to a cutting board to carve. Serve with the sausages, with the pan juices spooned over the top.

MOROCCAN CORNISH HENS *with* M'HAMSA

Serves 4 to 6

This is a fun and slightly more formal dish than the others in this book. The ingredients require some effort to procure, yet are certainly worth it and can be modified as follows: M'hamsa is a fantastic Tunisian hand-rolled, large-grain couscous with a toasted quality and a toothsome bite. Israeli couscous, which also has a large grain, and the more common and much smaller Moroccan couscous, can also be used in a similar fashion, though you may need to adjust cooking technique and timing accordingly. A sweet-tart blood orange is my preferred citrus for this dish but when they're unavailable, I use a juice orange instead. The heat of harissa varies with the brand. Add a little more or less than I call for, as you like. If you're not a fan of cilantro, parsley works well, too.

3 Cornish hens (about 1¼ to 1½ pounds each), halved lengthwise (see Box)

24 dry-cured pitted black olives (about a heaping ½ cup)

6 tablespoons unsalted butter, at room temperature

1 blood orange

½ cup plus 3 tablespoons finely chopped yellow onion

2 teaspoons harissa

2 tablespoons finely chopped fresh cilantro leaves, plus more for sprinkling

Fine sea salt

Freshly ground black pepper

3 tablespoons extra-virgin olive oil, plus more for drizzling

2 cups M'hamsa couscous

Flaky coarse sea salt

Preheat the oven to 500°F with the rack in the middle. Rinse the hen pieces, and pat dry all over very well. Use your fingers to gently loosen the skin from the meat.

Finely chop enough of the olives to make 3 tablespoons; roughly chop the rest. Put the finely chopped olives and butter in a bowl. Finely zest the orange into the bowl, holding the zester close so that you capture the flavorful oil that sprays from the orange as you zest. Add the 3 tablespoons onion to the bowl, the harissa, and cilantro; mix together to thoroughly combine. Into a separate bowl, squeeze the juice from the orange and set aside.

Spread the flavored butter under the skin of the hens, then pat the skin sides of the hens dry again and season well with fine sea salt and pepper.

Heat 1 tablespoon oil in a 12-inch heavy skillet over medium-high heat until hot but not smoking. Reduce the heat to medium and brown 3 hen halves, skin side-down, until golden, about 6 minutes. Transfer, skin-side up, to a large rimmed baking dish or baking sheet. Repeat with the remaining halves, without adding more oil to the skillet. Set aside.

Bring 3 cups water to a simmer; remove from the heat and cover to keep hot. Heat the remaining 2 tablespoons oil in a large Dutch oven over medium-high heat. Add the remaining ½ cup onion, reduce the heat to low, and cook, stirring occasionally, until softened, about

splitting hens

To split Cornish hens in half, use a sharp pair of kitchen shears or a sharp knife. With the breast-side down on a cutting board, cut along either side of the backbone, cutting close to the bone to avoid the meat, then cut through the breastbone.

5 minutes. Add the couscous and cook, stirring occasionally, until the couscous is lightly toasted and starts to make a popping sound, 3 to 5 minutes. Add the simmered water, bring to a boil, and remove the pan from the heat. Cover and let stand until the couscous is tender but still a bit firm to the bite, 10 to 12 minutes.

Meanwhile, roast the hens until cooked through, 13 to 15 minutes. Add the reserved orange juice and a generous pinch of coarse salt to the baking dish after removing the hens to a platter; heat to a simmer over high heat and cook for 1 minute, scraping up the pan bits.

Fluff the couscous, drizzle with a little oil, and season with coarse salt. Serve the hens with the couscous and pan juices, sprinkling the remaining chopped olives and cilantro on top.

ROAST CHICKEN *with* CHORIZO-LIME BUTTER

When you carve this succulent roast chicken, little pieces of chorizo from under the skin tumble onto the cutting board. Scoop them onto your serving plates, then bathe the bird and its bits with the tangy rich pan juices.

Serves 4

1 (4-pound) whole chicken

3 tablespoons unsalted butter, at room temperature

1 lime

2 ounces fully cooked Mexican or Spanish chorizo, cut into ⅛-inch cubes (see Box)

1 teaspoon dried oregano, preferably Greek

⅛ teaspoon cayenne pepper

1 small unpeeled yellow onion, quartered

Flaky coarse sea salt

Freshly ground black pepper

½ cup dry red wine

---

choosing chorizo

Most of the chorizo we find in the US is either Mexican or Spanish, and fully cooked. Mexican chorizo is seasoned with vinegar and chile peppers, while the Spanish sausage gets its flavor from garlic and sweet paprika. Drier air-cured chorizos are best sliced and eaten as an appetizer. Moister oven-cooked versions and fresh sausages are for cooking. I use Mexican cooking chorizo here.

Preheat the oven to 425°F with the rack in the middle. Pull off excess fat around the cavities of the chicken and discard, then rinse the chicken and pat dry very well, inside and out. From the edge of the cavity, slip a finger under the skin of each of the breasts, then gently but thoroughly loosen the skin from the meat of the breasts and thighs.

Put the butter in a bowl. Finely zest the lime into the bowl, holding the zester so that you capture the flavorful oil that sprays from the lime as you zest. Add the chorizo, oregano, and cayenne and mix together to thoroughly combine. Cut the lime in half, then cut the halves into quarters; set aside.

Working with about 1 tablespoon at a time, gently push the butter mixture into the spaces you created between the chicken skin and meat, being careful not to tear the skin. Gently rub your hand over the outside of the skin to smooth out the mixture and push it farther down between the skin and meat where you may not be able to reach with your hand.

Stuff the cavity of the bird with the onion quarters and the lime pieces, then tie the legs together with kitchen string. Season the chicken all over, using 2 to 3 teaspoons coarse salt and generous pepper.

Put a roasting pan (not nonstick) in the oven to heat for 10 minutes. Remove the pan from the oven and immediately put the chicken into the pan, breast-side up.

Roast for 15 minutes, then reduce the heat to 350°F and roast for 15 minutes more. Pour the wine over the chicken and continue to cook, basting with the juices every 20 minutes, until the juices run clear when the thigh is pierced with a fork, about 1 hour more.

Remove the pan from oven and transfer the chicken to a cutting board to rest for 5 minutes. Meanwhile, tilt the pan and spoon the fat from the pan juices and discard. Serve the chicken with the pan juices.

BERBERE-SPICED ROAST CHICKEN

Berbere is a complex, spicy, slightly astringent, and insanely delicious Ethiopian spice blend that includes chile, cumin, coriander, ginger, and ajowan. I like to play to its tangy quality by adding lemon zest and juice here.

Serves 4

1 large yellow onion, peeled, with root end intact

2 lemons

1 (4-pound) whole chicken

2 tablespoons extra-virgin olive oil

1 tablespoon berbere spice
(see Sources and Credits, page 170)

Fine sea salt

Freshly ground black pepper

Preheat the oven to 425°F with the rack in the middle. Cut the onion crosswise into ½-inch rings, keeping the slices intact. Lay the onion slices, overlapping if necessary, into the baking dish, skillet, or small roasting pan you are using to roast the chicken.

Into a medium bowl, finely zest the lemons, holding the zester close so you capture the flavorful oil that sprays from the lemons as you zest. Cut 1 lemon in half crosswise. Cut one of the lemon halves into quarters.

Pull off excess fat around the cavities of the bird and discard, then rinse the chicken and pat dry very well, inside and out. From the edge of the cavity, slip a finger under the skin of each of the breasts, then gently but thoroughly loosen the skin from the meat of the breasts and thighs. Over the sink or a plate, rub the chicken with the quartered pieces of lemon, then put the pieces into the cavity of the bird. Put the bird on top of the onions, breast-side up.

Squeeze 1½ tablespoons juice from the remaining lemons, and add to the bowl with the zest. Add the oil and berbere spice; whisk to combine.

Using your hands and working with 1 tablespoon of the spice mixture, gently push the mixture into the spaces you created between the chicken skin and meat of each breast, being careful not to tear the skin. As you work the mixture in, gently rub your hand over the outside of the skin to smooth out the mixture and push it farther down between the skin and meat. Tie the legs together with kitchen string. Rub 1 tablespoon of the mixture onto the bottom of the bird, then evenly rub the rest over the top. Season the chicken all over, using 2 teaspoons salt and generous pepper.

Roast for 15 minutes, then rotate the pan and reduce the heat to 350°F. Continue roasting, basting with the juices every 20 minutes, until the juices run clear when the thigh is pierced with a fork, about 1 hour more. Remove from the oven and let rest in the pan for 15 minutes, then baste with the juices.

Transfer the bird to a cutting board and let rest for 5 minutes, then carve and serve with the pan juices and onions.

PERUVIAN ROAST CHICKEN
with AVOCADO SALAD

Serves 4

An enameled cast-iron gratin dish or a heavy skillet is a nice choice for this bird, so that, after it's cooked, the sauce can be made in the same pan. If you like, you can soak the red onion for the salad in an ice-water bath for 10 minutes, then drain and pat dry before mixing with the rest of the ingredients. This takes away most of the bite.

1 (4-pound) whole chicken

1 lemon, cut into quarters

5 garlic cloves, finely chopped

Fine sea salt

3 tablespoons white vinegar

¼ cup plus 2 tablespoons white wine

2 tablespoons extra-virgin olive oil

2 tablespoons paprika

1½ tablespoons ground cumin

2 teaspoons freshly ground black pepper

½ teaspoon dried oregano

AVOCADO SALAD

2 firm-ripe avocados

½ to ¾ small red onion

¾ cup packed fresh cilantro leaves

2 tablespoons fresh lime juice

2 tablespoons extra-virgin olive oil

Flaky coarse sea salt

Pull off excess fat around the cavities of the chicken and discard, then rinse the chicken and pat dry very well, inside and out. Over the sink or a plate, rub the chicken with 2 of the lemon quarters; reserve the remaining 2 quarters. From the edge of the cavity, slip a finger under the skin of each of the breasts, then gently but thoroughly loosen the skin from the meat of the breasts and thighs.

Use the side of your knife and the blade to alternately chop and gently scrape the garlic and ½ teaspoon of fine salt together, until you have a garlic paste. Using your hands and working with a little bit of the paste at a time, gently push the paste into the spaces you created between the chicken skin and meat, being careful not to tear the skin. As you work the paste gently in, rub your hand over the outside of the skin to smooth out the paste and push it farther down between the skin and meat where you may not be able to reach with your hand.

In a small bowl, whisk together the vinegar, 2 tablespoons wine, oil, paprika, cumin, pepper, and oregano. Transfer the marinade to a 1-gallon resealable plastic bag, pressing out the excess air. Turn the bag over several times to distribute the marinade, then put it in a bowl in the refrigerator, turning occasionally, for at least 5 hours or up to 8 hours. Let the chicken stand at room temperature for 1 hour before cooking.

Preheat the oven to 425°F with the rack in the middle. Transfer the chicken from the bag to a baking dish and pour the marinade into a small bowl (turn the bag inside out, if necessary, and scrape any thick bits of spices into the bowl with the marinade). Squeeze the remaining lemon quarters into the cavity of the bird, put the squeezed rinds into the cavity, and tie the legs together with kitchen string. Season the chicken all over, using 1 teaspoon fine salt.

Roast the bird in the oven for 15 minutes, then baste with a bit of the marinade. Reduce the heat to 375°F and continue to roast, basting every 20 minutes with the marinade and the pan juices, until the juices of the chicken run clear when a thigh is pierced with a fork, about 1 hour and 15 minutes more.

Remove from the oven and let the chicken rest in the pan while you prepare the salad: Peel and cube the avocado. Very thinly slice as much onion as you want to use. Put the avocado, onion, cilantro, lime juice, oil, and a generous pinch of coarse salt in a bowl; set aside.

Transfer the chicken to a cutting board. Tip the pan so that you can see the oil separating from the pan juices; using a soupspoon, skim off and discard most of the oil. Bring the juices to a simmer over medium-high heat. Add the ¼ cup wine and, scraping any bits from the bottom and sides of the skillet, simmer for 3 minutes.

Toss the salad together. Carve the bird, and serve with the pan sauce and the salad.

ROAST JERK CHICKEN
with PINEAPPLE MINT SALAD

This is a dish that I love in both winter and summer. Its warming sweet spices heat up the cooler months, while its spicy chiles make for perfect summertime picnic fare.

Serves 4

½ cup chopped white onion

5 scallions, trimmed and roughly chopped

3 garlic cloves, peeled

1 (1-inch) piece fresh ginger, peeled

1 Scotch bonnet or habanero chile

2 tablespoons soy sauce

Fine sea salt

1½ teaspoons ground allspice

1 teaspoon freshly ground black pepper

½ teaspoon cinnamon

¼ teaspoon ground cloves

¼ teaspoon freshly grated nutmeg

¼ cup extra-virgin olive oil,
plus more for greasing

1 (4-pound) whole chicken, cut into
10 pieces (see page 9)

2 tablespoons fresh lime juice, plus lime
wedges for serving

PINEAPPLE MINT SALAD

¾ teaspoon whole black peppercorns

1 (3-pound) pineapple, cut into ¾-inch
cubes (4 cups)

1 tablespoon plus 2 teaspoons extra-virgin
olive oil

1 teaspoon flaky coarse sea salt

20 to 30 fresh mint leaves (2 to 3 sprigs)

2 scallions, trimmed and thinly sliced on a
long diagonal

In a food processor, purée the onion, scallions, garlic, ginger, chile, soy sauce, 1½ teaspoons fine salt, allspice, pepper, cinnamon, cloves, and nutmeg until smooth. With the machine running, slowly add the 1¼ cups oil.

Transfer the marinade to a 1-gallon resealable plastic bag. Add the chicken and seal the bag, pressing out the excess air. Turn the bag over several times to distribute the marinade, then put it into a bowl in the refrigerator, turning occasionally, for at least 2 hours or up to 1 day. Let the chicken stand at room temperature for 1 hour before cooking.

Preheat the oven to 450°F with the rack in the middle. Line a rimmed baking sheet with foil and add an oiled wire rack. Reserving the marinade, arrange the chicken pieces, skin-side up, in a single layer on the rack. Drizzle with the lime juice and season lightly with fine salt. Spoon the marinade over the chicken and roast until crisped on the edges and cooked through, 50 minutes to 1 hour (tenting with foil, if necessary, after 40 minutes).

Meanwhile, make the salad: In a mortar and pestle, or using the heel of your hand on the flat side of a chef's knife, coarsely crack the peppercorns. In a bowl, combine the pineapple and oil. Crushing it with your fingers, add the coarse salt, then add the cracked pepper and toss to combine. Add the mint and scallion and toss again; adjust the oil and seasoning, if necessary. Serve with the chicken.

> ### *hot, hot, hot*
>
> Like all ingredients, hot chile peppers can vary in intensity, even among the same variety. So any recipe that includes chiles—followed the same way twice—is likely to vary, too. The bulk of chile heat is in the seeds. If you're after very hot spice, include more than one pepper, though you may want to leave the seeds out. When handling spicy chiles, wear rubber gloves and/or wash your hands very well afterward. If you prefer milder dishes, make this dish with a less intense chile or with none at all. The complexity of the dish is present, even without the heat.

ROAST CHICKEN *with* SAFFRON, GINGER, *and* GOLDEN RAISINS

Can you assign a gender to a roast chicken? If the answer is yes, then this one is decidedly feminine. Its gorgeous floral aroma and flavor and pretty golden hue make it so. A simple pot of jasmine rice and lightly braised leeks make for equally graceful and delicious accompaniments.

Serves 4

1 (4-pound) whole chicken

4 tablespoons unsalted butter, at room temperature

1 orange

¼ cup golden raisins, soaked in boiling water to cover for 1 minute and drained

2 teaspoons grated fresh ginger

2 large garlic cloves, finely chopped

½ teaspoon saffron threads

½ teaspoon ground coriander

Flaky coarse sea salt

Freshly ground black pepper

1 cup dry white wine

Preheat the oven to 425°F with the rack in the middle.

Pull off excess fat around the cavities of the chicken and discard, then rinse the chicken and pat dry very well, inside and out. From the edge of the cavity, slip a finger under the skin of each of the breasts, then use your fingers to gently but thoroughly loosen the skin from the meat of the breasts and thighs.

Put the butter in a bowl. Finely zest the orange into the bowl, holding the zester close so that you capture the flavorful oil that sprays from the orange as you zest. Add the raisins, ginger, garlic, saffron, and coriander; mix together to thoroughly combine. Using your hands and working with about 1 tablespoon of the butter mixture at a time, gently push the mixture into the spaces you created between the chicken skin and meat, being careful not to tear the skin. As you work the mixture in, gently rub your hand over the outside of the skin to smooth out the mixture and push it farther down between the skin and meat where you may not be able to reach with your hand.

Tie the legs together with kitchen string, then season the chicken all over using 1 tablespoon coarse salt and generous pepper. Roast for 15 minutes, then pour the wine over the chicken, reduce the heat to 350°F, and continue to roast, basting every 15 minutes until the juices run clear when the thigh is pierced with a fork, about 1 hour and 15 minutes more. Transfer the chicken to a cutting board and let rest for 5 minutes, then carve. Serve with extra salt for sprinkling.

SWEET *and* SPICY KOREAN ROAST "BBQ" CHICKEN

Serves 4

I dubbed this bird "BBQ," since the barbecuing isn't done in the traditional Korean way (with a soy sauce–based marinade called *bulgogi*). Instead, I mix up a sauce using *kochujang*, a thick spicy pepper paste, which tastes very BBQ to me. Chicken wings work with this marinade, too. Use 4 pounds for this recipe.

½ cup plus 2 tablespoons *kochujang* (see Sources and Credits, page 170)

¼ cup sugar

2 tablespoons sesame oil

1½ tablespoons soy sauce

1½ tablespoons finely chopped fresh ginger

1 (4-pound) chicken, cut into 10 pieces (see page 9)

Olive oil for greasing

Flaky coarse sea salt

1 tablespoon sesame seeds

2 scallions, trimmed and thinly sliced on a long diagonal

In a large bowl, whisk together the *kochujang*, sugar, sesame oil, soy sauce, and ginger. Transfer the marinade to a 1-gallon resealable plastic bag. Add the chicken and seal the bag, pressing out the excess air. Turn the bag over several times to distribute the marinade, then put it in a bowl in the refrigerator, turning occasionally, for at least 12 hours or up to 1 day. Let the chicken stand at room temperature for 1 hour before cooking.

Preheat the oven to 425°F with the rack in the middle. Line a rimmed baking sheet with foil and add an oiled wire rack. Reserving the marinade, arrange the chicken pieces, skin-side up, in a single layer on the rack. Season lightly with salt.

Roast the chicken for 20 minutes, then brush with some of the reserved marinade. Reduce the heat to 350°F and cook for 20 minutes more. Brush with the remaining marinade and continue to cook the chicken, tenting with foil if the skin becomes too darkened, for 20 minutes more.

While the chicken is cooking, heat the sesame seeds in a small skillet over low heat, shaking the pan back and forth until the seeds are lightly golden, 3 to 5 minutes; transfer the seeds to a plate. Sprinkle the cooked chicken with the toasted sesame seeds and scallions to serve.

peeling, chopping, and storing fresh ginger

Fresh ginger can be tricky to peel and chop. For easy peeling, use the tip of a small spoon, with the inside facing you, and pull it toward you. To chop, thinly slice the ginger, then stack the slices and cut them into thin matchsticks, and chop. Wrap ginger in plastic and store it in a resealable plastic bag for up to 3 weeks in the fridge, or up to 2 months in the freezer.

TEA-BRINED FIVE-SPICE ROAST CHICKEN
with SPICY SESAME CUCUMBERS

This lacquered-looking, smoke-kissed, subtly sweet bird involves a little advance planning but it is otherwise easy and well worth the effort. The tea used is Lapsang Souchong, a robust, smoky Chinese type. Purchase it loose, if you can, since loose teas are generally better in quality than those in bags. A bowl of jasmine rice completes the meal. Save some leftover chicken to tuck into Chinese Roast Chicken Buns (page 169).

Serves 4

1 orange

⅓ cup loose Lapsang Souchong or Russian Caravan tea, or 12 tea bags

5 whole cloves

2 cinnamon sticks

2 whole star anise pods

1 teaspoon whole black peppercorns

1 teaspoon fennel seeds

3 slices fresh ginger (each about 1½ inches long and ⅛-inch thick)

½ cup kosher salt

¼ cup packed dark brown sugar

1 (4-pound) whole chicken

SPICY SESAME CUCUMBERS

1 tablespoon sesame seeds

1 medium to large cucumber, preferably a skinny one

¼ cup toasted sesame oil

¼ teaspoon red pepper flakes, plus more for serving

¼ teaspoon fine sea salt, plus more for serving

Granulated sugar

In a large saucepan, bring 8 cups of water to a boil. Meanwhile, using a sharp peeler or knife, cut the zest from the orange, avoiding the white pith. Spoon the tea into filter bags, or wrap in cheesecloth and tie with kitchen string to secure.

When the water comes to a boil, remove the pan from the heat. Add the zest, tea, cloves, cinnamon, star anise, peppercorns, fennel seeds, and ginger and let the mixture steep, uncovered and off the heat, for 20 minutes, then squeeze the liquid from the tea bags into the mixture and discard the bags. Add the kosher salt and brown sugar and stir to dissolve, then squeeze the juice from the orange into the mixture.

Pull off excess fat around the cavities of the chicken and discard. Rinse the chicken and put it into a 1-gallon resealable bag. Put the bag into a bowl, then pour the brine into the bag and seal the bag, pressing out any air. Put the bowl in the refrigerator and let the chicken sit in the brine, turning it a few times, for at least 12 hours and up to a day (the more time you have to let it sit, the deeper the flavor).

Remove the chicken from the brine and pat dry very well, inside and out. Arrange a wire rack to fit over a pan, place the bird in the pan, and refrigerate, uncovered, for 12 to 24 hours. (You can skip this step, but it's well worth the advance planning—given the fact that the bird is quite wet from the brine, this step gives you the crispiest skin.)

Preheat the oven to 450°F with the rack in the middle. Put an 8- to 10-inch cast-iron skillet, or heavy roasting pan, into the heated oven for 10 minutes. Meanwhile, remove the bird from the refrigerator and pat dry any dampness, inside and out. Tie the legs together with kitchen string.

Carefully remove the hot skillet from the oven and immediately place the bird, breast-side up, into the skillet and into the oven. Roast for

20 minutes, then turn the bird breast-side down. Roast for 20 minutes more, then turn the bird breast-side up again and continue to roast until the juices run clear when the thigh is pierced with a fork, about 20 minutes more (1 hour total). Let the chicken rest in the pan for 15 minutes.

While the bird is resting, prepare the cucumbers: Heat the sesame seeds in a small skillet over low heat, shaking the pan back and forth until the seeds are lightly golden, about 4 minutes. Remove the pan from the heat and let sit for a minute (the seeds will take on more color), then transfer the seeds to a plate to cool.

Trim the cucumber at each end, then create stripes by peeling lengthwise. Cut the cucumber crosswise into ¼-inch rounds. In a large bowl, whisk together the oil, pepper flakes, fine salt, and a pinch of sugar. Add the cucumber and toss evenly to coat. Use your hands to gently press each cucumber round into the pool of oil and spices in the bottom of the bowl so that each can pick up some of the salt. Transfer to a serving dish and use a spatula to drizzle all of the oil mixture over the cucumber.

Using a mortar and pestle (or a spare spice or pepper grinder), finely grind the toasted sesame seeds (seeds can be left whole, but have more flavor when ground). Sprinkle the seeds over the cucumbers, then sprinkle with salt and more pepper flakes, if desired. Serve the cucumbers with the carved bird.

have on hand

Tea filter bags, or kitchen string and muslin or cheesecloth for loose tea; a wire rack (a small rack is helpful so that you do not run into a space problem in the fridge) and a pan that will fit underneath it; a 1-gallon resealable bag. A cast-iron skillet is my pan of choice for this bird, but a heavy gratin, roasting pan, stainless-steel or enameled cast-iron skillet work well, too.

TANDOORI-*style* ROAST CHICKEN

Serves 4

This chicken may not have the bright red hue you find in many Indian and Pakistani restaurant versions (the color comes from spices, or, sometimes, food coloring), but its flavor is tandoori all the way. The marinade works well on chicken wings, too. This bird requires high-heat cooking, so make sure that your oven is clean before you start, or you may wind up with a smoky kitchen. You could serve this with Freekeh with Onions and Olive Oil (page 70), Green Rice (page 52) or plain rice, Roasted Cauliflower with Dry-Cured Black Olives and Parsley Leaves (page 65), or any kind of Indian side you like to make.

1 (4-pound) whole chicken

¾ cup plain 0% or 2% Greek yogurt

¼ cup fresh lemon juice

¼ cup finely chopped white onion

4 garlic cloves, finely chopped

2 tablespoons grated fresh ginger

2 teaspoons paprika

1½ teaspoons ground cumin

¾ teaspoon ground coriander

½ teaspoon cayenne pepper

¼ teaspoon turmeric

1 tablespoon flaky coarse sea salt

Olive oil for rack

Fine sea salt

Rinse the chicken under cold running water, then pat dry well. Cut into 10 pieces (see page 9), then make 2- to 3½-inch deep cuts in each piece. Put all of the chicken pieces into a 1-gallon resealable plastic bag.

In a large bowl, whisk together all of the remaining ingredients, except for the oil and fine sea salt. Transfer the marinade to the bag with the chicken, and seal the bag, pressing out the excess air. Turn the bag over several times to distribute the marinade, then put it into a bowl in the refrigerator, turning occasionally, for at least 6 hours or up to 1 day. Let the chicken stand at room temperature for 1 hour before cooking.

Preheat the oven to 450°F with the rack in the middle. Line a rimmed baking sheet with foil and add an oiled wire rack. One by one, transfer each chicken piece from the bag to the rack, skin-side up and in a single layer, letting any excess marinade drip back into the bag. Transfer the marinade to a bowl. Season the chicken with fine sea salt.

Put the pan on the lower rack and roast the chicken for 20 minutes, then brush with the marinade, transfer the pan to the upper rack, and continue cooking for 10 minutes more. Increase temperature to broil. Broil until cooked through and golden, 8 to 10 minutes.

Chapter two

WHAT'S on the SIDE

OLIVE OIL MASHED POTATOES *with* COARSE PEPPER *and* WISPY SCALLIONS

Serves 4

A forkful of juicy chicken and silky-smooth potato, swept through a pool of good olive oil, crunchy salt, crushed pepper, and wisps of sliced scallion, is heaven. A potato ricer (a handy tool that forces the cooked potato through a set of small holes, making it look like bits of rice) gives the mash a smooth texture. For a more rustic look and flavor, leave the skins on and mash with a fork instead.

2½ pounds Yukon gold potatoes, peeled and cut into 1-inch chunks

Flaky coarse sea salt

6 to 7 tablespoons good-quality extra-virgin olive oil, plus more for drizzling

2 scallions, trimmed and thinly sliced on a long diagonal

1 teaspoon whole black peppercorns, coarsely crushed in a mortar and pestle or with the flat side of a chef's knife

Put the potatoes and a pinch of salt in a large saucepan and fill with water. Bring the water to a boil and cook the potatoes until tender, 12 to 15 minutes.

Drain the potatoes, then transfer them to a large bowl and immediately mash with a fork, or put through a ricer. Stir in 1 tablespoon coarse salt, then, stirring until combined, drizzle in the oil. Serve warm with the scallions, extra salt, pepper, and an extra drizzle of oil on top.

oil for finishing

Higher-priced, good-quality extra-virgin olive oil is often referred to by chefs and food enthusiasts as "finishing oil," because it's the type you finish a dish or dress a salad with. Good oil is a must for this recipe, since the flavor is a key component of the dish. Finishing oils are often marked with the name of an estate, a vintage, and/or a "use by" date, stamped on the label, bottle, or bottleneck. Good-quality oils come from Italy, Spain, France, Greece, Morocco, South Africa, New Zealand, California, Chile, and beyond. They range in flavor from piquant to mellow, and in color from green to gold. I recommend tasting and keeping one to three good oils on hand, each with different characteristics. Use them up within a few months after opening. Heat and light are foes to all oils, so avoid those in clear glass, and store in a cool, dark place.

ROASTED POTATOES *with* COARSELY GROUND PEPPER, FRESH OREGANO, *and* GRANA PADANO CHEESE

Serves 4

Preheating a rimmed baking sheet in the oven, then carefully spreading uncooked, olive oil–bathed potato wedges on the hot surface, gives these spuds beautifully crispy edges.

2 pounds medium Yukon gold potatoes, cut lengthwise into ½-inch wedges

3 tablespoons extra-virgin olive oil

1 teaspoon flaky coarse sea salt, plus more for serving

½ cup (⅛-inch thick) shards freshly grated Grana Padano or Parmigiano-Reggiano cheese (about 2 ounces)

1½ tablespoons coarsely chopped fresh oregano leaves

½ teaspoon freshly ground coarse black pepper

Preheat the oven to 450°F with the rack in the middle.

Heat a rimmed baking sheet in the oven for 10 minutes. Meanwhile, in a large bowl, stir together the potatoes, oil, and salt.

Using oven mitts (it's easy to forget that the pan is hot), remove the pan from the oven and immediately spread the potatoes and their oil (using a rubber spatula to get all of the oil onto the pan) in a single layer onto the pan; reserve the bowl.

Roast the potatoes for 20 minutes then, using a metal spatula, loosen, stir, and turn the potatoes once. Continue roasting until golden and tender, 10 to 15 minutes more.

Remove from the oven and immediately transfer the potatoes to the reserved serving bowl. Add the cheese and oregano, tossing to combine. Add the pepper and more salt to taste.

SCALLOPED POTATOES *with* GOAT GOUDA *and* THYME

Serves 4 to 6

Variations on gratins seem endless, which is part of the fun of making them. Many gratins are made with heavy cream—tasty, no doubt, but I prefer a lighter dish, so I use a mix of milk and chicken broth instead. You can try different cheeses, or use none at all; swap thyme for other herbs; use a mix of potato types, or play with other root vegetables, like rutabaga, celery root, or winter squash. If you're not using an unsalted homemade broth, use a low-sodium type and decrease the amount of salt in this recipe by one-half or two-thirds (you can always add salt to taste, once the gratin is cooked, but the problem of too much salt can't be reversed). I like to really taste the black pepper, so I use a very coarse grind.

1 tablespoon unsalted butter for greasing pan

1¼ cups packed Goat Gouda, freshly grated on the fine holes of a grater (3 ounces)

2 pounds Yukon gold potatoes, cut crosswise into ⅛-inch-thick slices

1 garlic clove, thinly sliced

1½ teaspoons fine sea salt (use less if using store-bought broth, see Headnote)

¾ teaspoon freshly ground coarse black pepper

1 cup whole milk

1 cup chicken broth, preferably homemade (page 100)

1 teaspoon dried thyme

Preheat the oven to 400°F with the rack in the middle. Butter a 2-quart gratin or an 11x7x2-inch glass baking dish. Set aside ¼ cup of the cheese.

Arrange ⅓ of the potato slices in the bottom of the prepared dish, overlapping slightly and covering the bottom of the dish completely (you may have more than 1 layer). Sprinkle with ⅓ each of the remaining cheese, garlic, salt, and pepper. Repeat the layering process 2 more times.

In a large bowl, whisk together the milk and broth. Pour the mixture over the potatoes, then sprinkle with the thyme. Put the dish on a baking sheet and bake for 1 hour, then sprinkle with the reserved cheese and continue to bake until the potatoes are tender and the top is golden, 10 to 15 minutes more.

quick, even slicing

A mandolin-style adjustable-blade slicer is great for cutting potatoes and other root vegetables for gratins, and for making french fries and slaws. Inexpensive models can be found in urban Chinatown districts and online. Most come with a safety guard, which should always be used. It takes a little longer and pieces may be less uniform, but you can also slice the potatoes for this dish the old-fashioned way, using a good sharp knife.

POMMES FRITES *with* 3 MAYOS

Serves 4

A stack of crispy warm fries alongside a plateful of juicy roast chicken is one of life's great simple pleasures. Stir up your mayos first, to allow time for the flavors to blend. You can make all three, or prepare a double or triple batch of a single type. These are skinny shoestring-style fries, which cook quickly and don't require a double-fry.

GREEN GARLIC MAYO

½ teaspoon minced garlic

Fine sea salt

1 tablespoon finely chopped fresh herb leaves, such as basil, parsley, tarragon, chives, or chervil

3 tablespoons mayonnaise

SPICY MAYO

3 tablespoons mayonnaise

¼ to ½ teaspoon Sriracha or chile-garlic sauce (see Sources and Credits, page 170)

Generous pinch or two fine sea salt

SMOKED PAPRIKA MAYO

3 tablespoons mayonnaise

½ teaspoon fresh lemon juice

⅛ teaspoon Pimentón de la Vera (see Sources and Credits, page 170)

Generous pinch or two fine sea salt

POMME FRITES

2 pounds Idaho or russet potatoes, peeled, rinsed, and dried

1 quart vegetable oil

Flaky coarse sea salt

Freshly ground black pepper

To make the Green Garlic Mayo: Use the side of your knife and the blade to alternately chop and gently scrape the garlic and salt together, until you have a garlic paste. Stir the paste and herbs into the mayonnaise. Adjust the salt to taste.

To make the Spicy Mayo and the Smoked Paprika Mayo: In separate bowls, stir together all of the ingredients for each. Cover all 3 mayos and refrigerate while you make the frites.

Using an adjustable-blade slicer or chef's knife, cut the potatoes into ⅛-inch-thick slices. Pat the slices dry with paper towels, then, with a knife, cut them lengthwise into ⅛-inch-thick sticks. Cut the long sticks, from the center of the potato, in half. Thoroughly pat the potato sticks dry.

Line a baking sheet with paper towels.

In a deep skillet, heat 1½ inches of oil to 325°F in a 5-quart heavy pot over medium heat. In 5 batches, fry the potatoes until lightly golden (return oil to 325°F between batches), about 5 minutes per batch. Using a slotted spoon, transfer to the prepared baking sheet to drain. Season with coarse salt and pepper and serve with the mayos.

have on hand

A deep-fat thermometer, for gauging the heat of the frying oil; a baking sheet and paper towels, for draining the fries; plenty of good salt and freshly ground pepper for seasoning.

GREEN RICE

Serves 4

Raised in New York and Chicago, I was a city girl until the age of 13. That's when my parents, en route back to their native East Coast, chose country life in Hanover, NH, over a return to the Big Apple. Five acres of land complete with a small flock of sheep, a blackberry bramble, several rows of apple trees, and a rope swing that dropped my brother and I into the cool of a well-shaded swimming pond on hot August days replaced our suburban backyard grill and concrete pool. Mom planted rhubarb, blueberries, and copious fresh herbs. Her gardens were among the first inspirations of what became a farm-to-table way of life and my fulfilling food-related career. This dish is dedicated to her. It's a nice way to use up an excess of leftover herbs from the fridge, or perfect if you have your own garden to snip from.

5 scallions, trimmed

1½ tablespoons extra-virgin olive oil, plus more for drizzling

1 garlic clove, thinly sliced

1 cup jasmine rice

1 cup mixed chopped fresh herb leaves, such as basil, tarragon, mint, cilantro, chervil, and/or chives

Flaky coarse sea salt

Freshly ground black pepper

½ lemon, cut into 2 pieces and seeds removed

Thinly slice the scallions crosswise, keeping the whites and light green parts separate from the dark green parts.

Heat the oil in a medium saucepan over medium heat. Add the white and light green parts of the scallions and the garlic; reduce the heat to low and cook, stirring occasionally, until softened, about 5 minutes. Add the rice and 1½ cups of water and cook as directed on the package, until just tender and most of the liquid is absorbed.

Remove the rice from the heat, stir in the scallion greens and herbs, and season generously with salt and pepper. Drizzle with oil and squeeze the lemon over the top to taste.

POLENTA *with* TRUFFLED CHEESE

Serves 4

On the way to a friend's place for dinner early on New Year's Eve, Steve and I stopped to pick up cheeses and discovered Sottocenere, a full yet delicately flavored truffled cheese from the northern Italian region of Veneto. Other truffled cheeses, or any semisoft melting cheese, like Fontina, can be used in its place. Don't skip the Parmigiano-Reggiano, though, which adds a required high note with its richness, tang, and salt.

1 garlic clove, finely chopped

Fine sea salt

1¼ cups polenta (coarse cornmeal)

1¼ cups packed coarsely grated Sottocenere or other semisoft truffled cheese, or fontina (about 5 ounces)

⅓ cup freshly grated Parmigiano–Reggiano cheese (about 1½ ounces)

Freshly ground black pepper

Combine 5½ cups of water, garlic, and ¾ teaspoon salt in a heavy large saucepan and bring to a boil over high heat. In a slow, steady stream, whisk in the polenta. Reduce the heat to medium–low and simmer, stirring the polenta frequently with a long-handled wooden spoon, until it is thickened and creamy, about 20 minutes.

Stir in the cheeses, and season with salt and pepper.

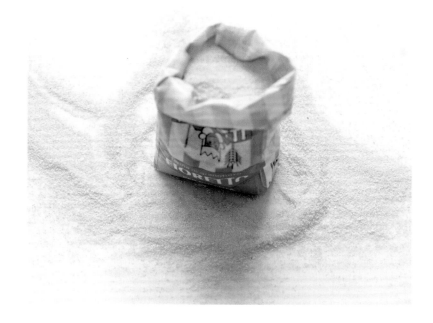

WILTED SPINACH *and* CHARD

Serves 4

A sauté of dark leafy greens is among the most beautiful and healthy of side dishes. This pure and simple version (sans garlic, chile, or lemon—though all are nice) allows the taste of the olive oil to be very present on the palate, which is the way I like it best. The oil and moisture from the greens create flavorful juices that blend nicely with simple mashed potatoes, if that happens to be on your plate, too. Use your favorite finishing oil (see Box on page 47) for drizzling once you've taken the greens off the heat.

1½ pounds red Swiss chard (about 1 large bunch)

½ to ¾ pound spinach (about 1 large bunch), tough stems and any wilted leaves discarded

¼ cup extra-virgin olive oil, plus more for drizzling

Flaky coarse sea salt

Cut the stems and center ribs from the chard, discarding any tough portions. Cut the remaining stems and ribs crosswise into 1-inch pieces. Roughly chop the chard leaves. Wash the chard and spinach and partially spin-dry, leaving some moisture on the leaves for cooking.

Heat the oil in a 5- to 6-quart Dutch oven or other heavy pot over medium heat, just until fragrant, then add the greens (in batches if necessary) and a generous pinch of salt. Cover and cook for 1 minute, then stir. Continue to cook, covered, stirring every minute or so, until wilted and tender, 3 to 4 minutes total.

Transfer the greens to a serving plate, spoon some of the juices from the pot over the top, season lightly with salt, and drizzle with oil.

WARM SUGAR SNAP PEAS *with* MINT

The simplest recipes are the best when it comes to understanding technique and ingredients. Here, the warmth of just-cooked snap peas releases the aroma and flavor of the olive oil. The peas are then cooled before adding the mint so that the mint leaves stay spry and bright. Choose a good olive oil for finishing (one you like the flavor of) and a flaky coarse sea salt (the one you love best for taste and texture). The special qualities of each ingredient are notable in the finished dish. You don't have to shell any of the peas, but the variety of shapes looks nice if you do.

Good basic kitchen salt, like kosher (for water)

1 pound sugar snap peas, strings removed

3 tablespoons good-quality extra-virgin olive oil

2 teaspoons flaky coarse sea salt, plus more for serving

¼ cup loosely packed fresh mint leaves, preferably small and medium ones

Bring a medium saucepan of well-salted water to a boil. Add the peas and cook until just tender, 1 to 2 minutes (the peas will continue to cook as they cool). Drain and transfer to a large bowl. Immediately add the oil and coarse salt and toss to combine, then let the peas sit for a few minutes to cool.

Split 10 to 15 pea pods, shelling the peas and adding the shelled peas with their shells back to the bowl. Add half of the mint leaves and toss. Transfer to a serving bowl, using a rubber spatula to get all of that good oil into the bowl.

Sprinkle with coarse salt and the remaining mint. Serve warm or at room temperature.

ASPARAGUS, MUSHROOMS, *and* PEAS *with* LEMON *and* TARRAGON

Serves 4

Combining sweet asparagus and peas with the earthy flavor of mushrooms and the floral, licorice notes of tarragon creates an interesting and delicious dish. A mix of mushrooms is nice, and you can use any cultivated or wild types you like. Mint or basil can be substituted for tarragon. I like the tender bite of not-too-done asparagus so I cook the spears briefly in boiling water before they go into the skillet. If you prefer them cooked more, boil for an extra 2 minutes or so.

Good basic kitchen salt, like kosher (for water)

1 pound asparagus, trimmed and cut crosswise into thirds

2 tablespoons extra-virgin olive oil

2 tablespoons unsalted butter

½ pound button mushrooms, stems trimmed and halved or quartered, if large

4 ounces shiitake mushrooms (about 5 large), stems trimmed, caps cut in half, or quartered, if large

Flaky coarse sea salt

2 tablespoons finely chopped shallot (about 1 large)

1 cup fresh or frozen peas

1 lemon

2 teaspoons finely chopped fresh tarragon leaves

Freshly ground coarse black pepper

Bring a large saucepan of well-salted water to a boil. Add the asparagus and cook for 1 minute if the stalks are skinny, or 2 to 4 minutes if they are a medium or fat thickness. Drain and run under cold water to stop cooking, then gently pat dry.

Heat the oil and 1 tablespoon of the butter in a large nonstick skillet over medium-high heat. Add the mushrooms and cook until golden on bottom sides, 2 to 3 minutes, then stir and cook until golden all over and tender but not softened, 1 to 2 minutes more. Transfer to a large serving bowl and sprinkle with a pinch of coarse salt.

Add the remaining 1 tablespoon butter and shallot to the skillet, then add the asparagus, peas, and a generous pinch of coarse salt. Return the skillet to medium-high heat and cook, tossing once or twice, until the vegetables are tender but still firm to the bite, about 2 minutes. Transfer the mixture to the bowl with the mushrooms. While the vegetables are hot, finely zest the lemon into the bowl, holding the zester close so that you capture the flavorful oil that sprays from the lemon as you zest. Add the tarragon and toss to combine. Season with coarse salt and pepper.

CORN ON THE COB *with* OLIVE OIL *and* CRACKED BLACK PEPPER

Serves 4

I've been slathering corn on the cob with good olive oil for years, all the while thinking my fondness for the duo, though nice, was probably not worth a written recipe. Then one summer, when our friend Linda Wilkinson exclaimed that the pairing was "beyond," I promised the dish would make it into a cookbook one day. This dish works best when you use a good-quality finishing oil—whether fruity, grassy, peppery, subtle, assertive, that's up to you—and a liberal sprinkling of both crunchy sea salt and freshly cracked coarse pepper.

Good basic kitchen salt, like kosher (for water)

4 ears corn, shucked

½ to 1 teaspoon whole black peppercorns

4 to 6 tablespoons good-quality extra-virgin olive oil

Flaky coarse sea salt

Bring a large pot of well-salted water to a boil. Add the corn and cook until just tender, 4 to 5 minutes.

Meanwhile, using a mortar or pestle or the heel of your hand on the side of a chef's knife, coarsely crack the peppercorns.

Using tongs, transfer the corn to a platter. Immediately drizzle with oil and sprinkle with salt and pepper. Serve warm or at room temperature.

salting the water

Save your specialty salts for sprinkling over cooked dishes and salads. For salting boiling water for pasta, corn, and other vegetables, using a good basic kitchen salt, like kosher, does the trick.

ROASTED RADICCHIO *and* ONIONS

Serves 4

A simple pairing of flavor opposites is often a big hit. Sweet onions are a perfect foil for pleasingly bitter radicchio, which, when roasted, becomes deliciously crisp at the edges. I love this dish warm, room temperature, and even cold, and I always make extra. The leftovers are fantastic warm with loosely scrambled eggs for brunch, layered on sandwiches, or tossed into a pasta; they're also tasty as a snack enjoyed right out of the fridge.

2 medium heads radicchio (about 1¼ pounds total)

2 medium yellow onions

6 tablespoons extra-virgin olive oil

Flaky coarse sea salt

Freshly ground black pepper

Preheat the oven to 400°F with the racks positioned in the middle and upper third of the oven. Line 2 baking sheets with parchment paper.

Cut each head of radicchio in half, then cut the halves into 6 wedges each, keeping the ends intact. Cut the onions in the same manner.

Arrange the radicchio wedges, cut-side down and overlapping slightly, on 1 baking sheet. Drizzle with 4 tablespoons of the oil and season with 1 teaspoon salt and generous pepper.

Arrange the onions, cut-side down, on the second baking sheet in the center of the pan (onions placed too close to the edges may burn). Drizzle with the remaining 2 tablespoons oil and season with ¾ teaspoon salt and generous pepper.

Roast, rotating and swapping the baking sheets from the upper to middle racks halfway through, until the radicchio is browned and softened, with crisp edges, and the onions are golden and tender, 30 to 35 minutes.

ROASTED PARSNIPS *with* ZA'ATAR *and* ALEPPO PEPPER

Serves 4

Za'atar and Aleppo pepper are extraordinary spices and worthy additions to the larder. Za'atar is a Lebanese blend of thyme, sesame seeds, sumac, and salt. Aleppo pepper—a sweet-hot pepper grown in Syria and Turkey—is sun-dried, then ground. Sprinkle Aleppo on anything you want to add a little heat to. Both spices are great on everything from vegetables and pizzas to chicken, fish, and more. If you're buying loose parsnips for this dish, choose ones that are similar in size. Small to medium are best for this cutting style, since they're more uniform in width than the large ones, which tend to have very fat tops and much skinnier tips.

2 teaspoons za'atar, plus more for sprinkling (see Sources and Credits, page 170)

¼ teaspoon Aleppo pepper, plus more for sprinkling (see Sources and Credits, page 170)

½ teaspoon flaky coarse sea salt, plus more for sprinkling

2 pounds parsnips

2 tablespoons extra-virgin olive oil

Preheat the oven to 425°F with the rack in the middle.

In a small bowl, mix together the za'atar, Aleppo pepper, and salt.

Peel the parsnips, cut them in half lengthwise (if you have very fat ones, cut them into quarters), and, in a bowl, toss them with the oil and the spice mixture to coat. Arrange the parsnips in a single layer on a rimmed baking sheet. Roast for 20 minutes, then toss and stir the parsnips. Continue roasting until golden and tender, 10 to 15 minutes more.

Remove from the oven and sprinkle with more of the spices and salt to taste. Serve warm or at room temperature.

---

cutting long and slender parsnips

Cutting long vegetables (like parsnips and carrots) lengthwise looks beautiful but can be awkward, depending on both the quality of your knife and the shape of the particular vegetable. To keep it beautiful, safe, and easy, use a well-sharpened knife and, instead of trying to cut the entire length of the vegetable in one fell swoop, hold the knife in line with the parsnip and cut from the middle to the fatter end first, then turn the vegetable and cut from the middle to the skinny end.

GIGANTE BEANS *with* KALE

Canned beans simply don't come close in flavor to dried. Inexpensive and easy to cook, dried beans do require a soak, but once they're on the stove, they are virtually fuss-free. Make this recipe a day or two ahead, if you can, as the flavors deepen markedly over time. Leftovers can be eaten with their cooking liquid as a soup, mashed and then spread onto crusty bread, or spooned alongside browned sausages.

Serves 4 to 6

**1 pound dried gigante beans
(about 3 cups)**

1 head garlic, unpeeled

**2 large leafy sprigs sage, rosemary,
or a combination**

**1 crumbled dried arbol chile,
or ¼ teaspoon red pepper flakes,
or ½ teaspoon whole black peppercorns**

**1 (½-pound) bunch kale, stems and center
ribs discarded and leaves coarsely chopped**

Flaky coarse sea salt

Good-quality extra-virgin olive oil

Freshly ground black pepper

Rinse the beans. Wrap the garlic, sage, and chile in cheesecloth and tie with kitchen string to secure. Place in a large saucepan, add the beans, and cover with cold water by 3 inches. Soak for 8 hours, or overnight.

Place the pot over medium heat, and bring to a boil then reduce to a very gentle simmer and cook the beans, adding water as needed to keep the water level about 2 inches above the beans, until the beans are tender, 1½ to 2 hours. (If you're not serving right away, let the beans cool down in their liquid, then put the beans and their liquor into an airtight container and refrigerate. The beans and their liquor can be reheated over medium heat.)

In small handfuls, gently stir the kale into the beans, adding more greens once the previous addition is wilted (add water as needed to keep level just above the greens and beans). Once all the kale is in the pot, add water as necessary, to just cover the greens and beans, and 2 teaspoons salt. Return the liquid to a simmer and cook until the kale is tender, 5 to 8 minutes, then remove and discard the sachet of aromatics.

To serve, transfer to a serving bowl using a slotted spoon. Add a few splashes of the bean liquor, a generous drizzle of olive oil, and a sprinkle of salt and pepper.

---

key to good bean cookery

The most important thing to understand when it comes to beans is that age determines cooking time. The older the beans, the longer they will take to cook. Though it can be hard to determine the age of the beans you buy, even older beans won't cause a problem once you get into the kitchen. If the beans are not done after an hour or so, keep cooking, adding more water as necessary, until they are tender. To get the best quality beans available, look for beans with a "use by" date, and/or purchase from a reputable shop that moves product quickly (see Sources and Credits, page 170).

ROASTED CAULIFLOWER *with* DRY-CURED BLACK OLIVES *and* PARSLEY LEAVES

Sweet roasted cauliflower, salty, earthy olives, and bitter parsley create a nice play of both color and flavor in this dish. The core of the cauliflower is edible. Instead of discarding it, trim it, then cut it into pieces similar in size to the florets. As is often my preference, I like to coarsely grind my pepper here, but you can grind it however you like.

Serves 4

1 large head cauliflower (2½ to 3 pounds)

¼ cup plus 1 tablespoon extra-virgin olive oil

¼ teaspoon flaky coarse sea salt

Aleppo pepper or freshly ground black pepper, or a combination

½ cup fresh flat-leaf parsley leaves

⅓ cup coarsely chopped pitted dry-cured black olives

Preheat the oven to 400°F with the rack in the middle. Line a rimmed baking sheet with parchment paper.

Cut the cauliflower into 1½-inch-wide florets; cut the core into equal-sized pieces. Toss with the oil, salt, and generous pinch pepper in a large bowl. Arrange the cauliflower in a single layer on the baking sheet. Roast, tossing occasionally, until golden and tender, 40 to 45 minutes.

Meanwhile, combine the parsley and olives in a large serving bowl.

Remove the pan from the oven and, while the cauliflower is hot, transfer to the bowl with the parsley and olives. Toss to combine and season with pepper to taste.

FARRO *with* SPICY SUN-DRIED TOMATO SPREAD *and* FETA CHEESE

Serves 4

Farro is a nutrient-rich grain, related to spelt. Its nutty taste and toothsome texture is perfect for side dishes, salads, and risottos (or rather, "farrotos," see page 132). Some recipes soak the grain before cooking it, and others require a much longer cooking time. The easy, non-soak cooking method here is the one I've always used (whether the farro is pearled, meaning the hull has been removed, or not, which may require a few more minutes of cooking time). This quick recipe also uses a favorite pantry item: spicy Tunisian sun-dried tomato spread.

Good basic kitchen salt, like kosher (for water)

1½ cups dried farro (about 10 ounces)

3 tablespoons good-quality extra-virgin olive oil

1 lemon

Scant ½ cup sheep's milk feta cheese, crumbled (2½ ounces)

1 to 2 tablespoons spicy sun-dried tomato spread (see Box below and Sources and Credits, page 170)

⅓ cup roughly chopped fresh flat-leaf parsley leaves, packed

Flaky coarse sea salt

Bring a medium saucepan of well-salted water to a boil. Add the farro and cook until tender but still firm to the bite, about 18 minutes. Drain and transfer to a bowl.

Add the oil, then finely zest the lemon into the bowl, holding the zester close so that you capture the flavorful oil that sprays from the lemon as you zest. Toss to thoroughly combine.

Add the cheese, 1 tablespoon sun-dried tomato spread, parsley, and a few generous pinches of salt. Stir to combine thoroughly. Allow the flavors to meld for a couple of minutes, then taste and adjust the amounts of sun-dried tomato spread and salt to your liking.

Serve warm or at room temperature.

> *make your own spicy sun-dried tomato spread*
>
> Les Moulins Mahjoub spicy sun-dried tomato spread is a blend of sun-dried tomatoes, olive oil, piment d'Espelette (a French chile, widely used in Basque kitchens), garlic, and coriander. If you want to make your own similar spread, you can finely chop and mix together the ingredients above, seasoning with salt and pepper, or substitute ingredients, using any fresh or dried chile you like, and one or a mix of fresh herbs. If you are using sun-dried tomatoes that do not come packed in oil, then stir the paste together with good-quality extra-virgin olive oil to moisten. For those that do come packed in oil, drain them first, then use a good-quality oil in your mix, if extra moistening is required.

ROASTED RED *and* GOLDEN BEETS *with* BASIL

Serves 4 to 6

Oh, it makes me sad to hear people say they "hate" beets. Beets are candy-sweet, gorgeous deliciousness. The matter of liking them is often more a matter of understanding how to prepare them than anything else. Using both red and golden beets brings added color to the table, but you can make this dish with a single variety, depending on your whim or what's available.

2 pounds red and golden beets (about 8 medium), greens trimmed, leaving about ¼ inch of the stem

6 tablespoons red wine vinegar

Flaky coarse sea salt

Freshly ground coarse black pepper

Sugar, optional

5 tablespoons extra-virgin olive oil

Leaves from 1 small bunch fresh basil

Preheat the oven to 400°F with the rack in the middle.

Put the beets in a baking dish and add water to come up about ½ inch. Cover the baking dish tightly with foil and roast the beets until they can be easily pierced through to the center with a knife or skewer, 45 minutes to 1 hour or more, depending on size. Uncover, remove from the oven, and allow the beets to cool.

Trim and discard the beet tops and tails, then peel the beets. Cut the red beets into halves, quarters, or sixths, depending on their size, and transfer to a bowl. Do the same with the orange beets, putting them into a separate bowl (otherwise the colors will bleed). Add 1 tablespoon vinegar to each bowl and a generous pinch of salt and pepper. If the beets are at all bitter, add a pinch of sugar. Toss to combine. Let the beets absorb the vinegar for 10 minutes.

In a bowl, whisk together the remaining 4 tablespoons vinegar and the oil. Transfer the beets to plates and spoon the dressing over the top. Arrange the basil leaves on the plates. Season generously with salt.

FREEKEH *with* ONIONS *and* OLIVE OIL

Serves 4

I recently discovered freekeh (pronounced free-ka), a nutrient-rich, rice-like grain at my local farmers' market. The first time I made it, I loved its nutty and somewhat smoky flavor so much, I heated up the leftovers for both breakfast and lunch every day afterward until I had eaten it all up. This is a versatile side that works well with a range of flavors and can be used as the base for a freekeh salad.

2 cups freekeh (see Sources and Credits, page 170)

Flaky coarse sea salt

4 tablespoons extra-virgin olive oil

¾ cup coarsely chopped yellow onion

2 garlic cloves, thinly sliced

Aleppo pepper or freshly ground black pepper

In a medium saucepan, combine 4¾ cups water, freekeh, 1½ teaspoons salt, and 1 tablespoon oil. Bring to a boil over high heat, then reduce to a simmer and cook, covered, until the freekeh is tender but still toothsome, and the water is absorbed, 40 to 45 minutes.

Meanwhile, in a small saucepan, combine the remaining 3 tablespoons oil, onion, garlic, and a generous pinch of salt and pepper. Heat over low heat, until warm and fragrant, 6 to 8 minutes, then remove from the heat and set aside.

When the freekeh is ready, gently reheat the oil mixture, just to warm through, then stir into the freekeh to thoroughly combine. Season with salt and pepper to taste. Serve warm or at room temperature.

GREEK LENTIL *and* RICE PILAF

Serves 4

This delicious Greek side makes a nice twosome with chicken, whether your bird is cooked in a Greek style or not. Use small lentils—French Puy, Spanish pardina, or Italian castellucio or colfiorito—these types are firm-tender, not mushy, and hold their shape once cooked. If you have fresh parsley, cilantro, or chives on hand, a sprinkle just before serving lends a nice extra touch.

1 cup small green or brown lentils, sorted of debris and rinsed

¼ cup extra-virgin olive oil

2 cups finely chopped yellow onions (about 1 large)

2 garlic cloves, finely chopped

1 tablespoon dried oregano, preferably Greek (see Sources and Credits, page 170)

2 teaspoons ground coriander

½ teaspoon ground allspice

¾ cup jasmine rice

Fine sea salt

1 tablespoon honey

1 tablespoon red wine vinegar

Freshly ground black pepper

Greek yogurt for serving, optional

In a medium saucepan, combine 2½ cups water and lentils. Bring to a boil over high heat, then reduce to a simmer and cook, covered, stirring occasionally, until the lentils are tender yet still firm to the bite, 20 to 25 minutes. Drain and spread the cooked lentils on a plate to cool.

In a 12-inch skillet, heat the oil over medium-high heat. Add the onions, garlic, oregano, coriander, and allspice. Reduce the heat to medium and cook, stirring occasionally, until softened, about 7 minutes. Add the rice and cook, stirring, until the rice is toasted and looks opaque, about 2 minutes more.

Stir in 1¾ cups water and 1 teaspoon salt; bring to a boil over high heat, then reduce to a simmer and cook, stirring occasionally, until the rice is tender and the liquid is absorbed, 13 to 15 minutes.

Meanwhile, whisk together the honey and vinegar.

When the rice is cooked, stir in the lentils and honey mixture; cook 1 minute more. Season generously with pepper, then adjust salt to taste. Serve with yogurt, if desired.

Chapter three

ROAST CHICKEN SALADS

BIBB, SWEET TURNIP, ROAST CHICKEN, *and* LEMON SALAD

Serves 4

Salad turnips, also known as Japanese turnips, are sweet, crisp, mild white beauties that crop up at markets in spring and fall. They are delicious raw in salads, or quickly sautéed or blanched. Their tender greens are terrific cooked in a skillet with a little olive oil, for a side dish, or to toss into rice dishes or pastas. No need to peel the little bulbs, just rinse, wipe dry, and eat.

¾ pound Bibb lettuce (about 2 heads) or Boston lettuce (about 1 head), leaves separated, torn if large

1 bunch salad turnips, trimmed and cut into halves, quarters, or sixths, depending on size

3 tablespoons good-quality extra-virgin olive oil, plus more for drizzling

2½ tablespoons fresh lemon juice

Flaky coarse sea salt

1½ cups sliced roast chicken

10 to 12 chives, cut into ½-inch lengths

Freshly ground black pepper

Toss together the lettuce, turnips, oil, lemon juice, and a generous pinch or two of salt in a large bowl.

Transfer the salad to a serving platter or onto individual plates. Tuck the chicken slices between the leaves. Drizzle the chicken with a little oil, then sprinkle the whole salad with the chives and more salt and pepper to taste.

---

bibb, boston, and butterhead

The "B" lettuces are known sometimes to cause confusion. Both Bibb and Boston are butterhead (or simply "butter") lettuces, Boston being the larger of the two. Both have sweet, tender leaves.

WINTER ROAST CHICKEN SALAD *with* FENNEL, BLOOD ORANGE, *and* PISTACHIO

Serves 4

This salad is evidence that beauty and simplicity can come together on a plate in a matter of minutes. It's best with a tart-sweet citrus, but if blood oranges aren't available, try Cara Cara oranges or one or two pink grapefruits instead.

3 blood oranges

2 medium fennel bulbs, trimmed, fronds reserved

1½ cups medium shreds roast chicken

3½ tablespoons red wine vinegar

3 tablespoons good-quality extra-virgin olive oil

Flaky coarse sea salt

3 tablespoons shelled unsalted pistachios, roughly chopped

Using a sharp paring knife, trim off the tops and bottoms of the oranges. Stand 1 orange on end and carefully cut the peel and pith from the flesh, following the curve of the fruit from the top to the bottom. Work your way around the fruit to peel on all sides. Cut both sides of each section away from the membranes, and place in a large bowl. Squeeze any juice from the membranes into the bowl. Repeat with the remaining blood oranges.

Cut fennel bulbs in half lengthwise, and slice very thinly. Add the fennel, chicken, vinegar, and oil to the bowl with the orange sections, then gently toss together.

Coarsely chop some of the fennel fronds. Arrange the salad on a platter, season generously with salt, and sprinkle with the pistachios and fronds.

CHERRY TOMATO, CRISP RADISH, *and* TOASTED BREAD SALAD *with* SHREDDED ROAST CHICKEN *and* FRESH HERBS

Serves 4 to 6

Make this version of Italian bread salad (or *panzanella*) with the ripest local tomatoes you can get your hands on, and you will see that it is summer in a bowl. The tomatoes are a must, but the other vegetables are flexible. Use celery in place of radish, if you like, or add blanched green beans or boiled or roasted corn, cut off the cob.

⅔ cup very thinly sliced red onion (about 1 small)

4 cups cubed (¾-inch) rustic bread (about 5 ounces)

1 garlic clove, finely chopped

Fine sea salt

½ cup extra-virgin olive oil

2 tablespoons red wine vinegar

1½ pounds cherry tomatoes, halved

1 medium cucumber

4 small or 2 large radishes

2 cups shredded roast chicken

1 cup packed fresh basil leaves

½ cup packed fresh flat-leaf parsley leaves

2 tablespoons capers, preferably salt-packed, rinsed, soaked in cold water for 10 minutes, then rinsed again and minced

Flaky coarse sea salt

Preheat the oven to 450°F with the rack in the middle. Put the onion in a bowl and cover with 1 to 2 cups of cold water. Swish the water around and rub the slices with your hand. Drain and repeat the process two or three times, letting the slices soak and changing the water every 10 minutes or so.

Spread out the bread cubes on a rimmed baking sheet and bake until the edges are crisp and golden, 6 to 8 minutes. Cool completely.

Peel and cut the cucumber into ½-inch cubes. Thinly slice the radishes. Drain the onion slices and pat dry well.

Use the side of your knife and the blade to alternately chop and gently scrape the garlic and a generous pinch of fine salt together, until you have a garlic paste. Put the oil and vinegar in a bowl. Add the garlic paste and whisk to combine.

Put the cooled bread, tomatoes, and a generous pinch of fine salt in a large bowl and toss to combine, gently pressing the tomatoes a bit to release some of the juices.

Place all in a large serving bowl, then add the bread mixture, chicken, basil, parsley, and capers. Toss to combine. Whisk together the garlic paste dressing, add to the salad, and toss once more. Season with coarse salt.

> ## relishing the raw
> If uncooked onions send you running, read on. The technique of soaking and rinsing an onion takes away the "raw bite," pulling the vegetable's sweetness to the forefront. Once dressed, the onions become pickled or "cooked" by the vinegar; they hardly taste raw at all.

RED QUINOA SALAD *with* ROAST CHICKEN, TART APPLE, GROUND PEPPER, *and* FRESH BASIL

Serves 4

Tiny quinoa—what the little grain lacks in size it more than makes up for with its fresh, nutty flavor and impressive nutritional "cred." Deemed a supergrain, quinoa is rich in antioxidants, easy-to-digest fiber, and immune-system-boosting amino acids. It's also extremely high in protein, as well as wheat-free, gluten-free, and quick and easy to cook. Red quinoa is heartier tasting than white, but both varieties are light and fluffy, and either can be used here.

1 cup pre-washed red quinoa (see Box)

2 cups small shreds roast chicken

1 Granny Smith apple, cut into ⅛-inch slices, then into 1-inch-long matchsticks

½ cup thinly sliced fresh basil leaves

2 scallions, trimmed and thinly sliced on a long diagonal

6 tablespoons fresh lemon juice

3 tablespoons extra-virgin olive oil

1 teaspoon fine sea salt

Freshly ground black pepper

In a medium saucepan, combine 2 cups of water and quinoa. Bring to a boil over high heat, then reduce to a simmer and cook, covered, until the water is absorbed, about 15 minutes. Spread the cooked quinoa on a plate to cool.

In a large bowl, toss together the cooled quinoa, chicken, apple, basil, and scallions. Add the lemon juice, oil, and salt, and toss once more. Season with pepper.

---

rinsing quinoa

Quinoa can be purchased packaged or in bulk bins. If your quinoa has not been fully cleaned and rinsed (the package or bin will say, if so), rinse it well before cooking to remove the off-tasting coating of saponin, which the plant naturally produces to keep birds and insects at bay.

ROAST CHICKEN and THICK-SLICED SUMMER TOMATOES with SPANISH OLIVE OIL and FRESH HERBS

Serves 4

This is the best kind of lazy-summer-day dish. It's ready in minutes and is beautiful, easy, and ridiculously satisfying. Any single variety or mix of type, size, or shape of tomatoes works—as long as they're fully ripe and, when cut into, brimming with juice. I specify Castillo de Canena, a fruity Spanish extra-virgin olive oil, because it's among my all-time favorites and the one I like best for this recipe. But great olive oil can be had from all sorts of places, and you can use whatever you like.

1 teaspoon whole black peppercorns

12 to 14 slices roast chicken★

1¼ to 1½ pounds tomatoes, in season and preferably local for best quality, thickly sliced

Castillo de Canena extra-virgin olive oil (see Sources and Credits, page 170)

A small handful of fresh chives, cut into 1½-inch lengths

A handful of fresh basil leaves

Flaky coarse sea salt

★From 1 (3½- to 4-pound) bird

In a mortar and pestle or, using the heel of your hand on the flat side of a chef's knife, coarsely crack the peppercorns.

Arrange the chicken and tomatoes on each of four plates. Drizzle generously with oil, then sprinkle with the chives, basil, crushed peppercorns, and salt.

ROAST CHICKEN SALAD *with* TOASTED WALNUTS, GRAPES, *and* CELERY LEAVES

Serves 4

Walnuts, grapes, and celery are classic chicken salad companions. To perk up the dish, and to provide a counterpoint to the sweetness of the grapes, I add two types of herbs, plus whole celery leaves, which lend a beautiful and very herby character, as well. Try smoked or Marcona almonds (not toasted), toasted pistachios, or roasted peanuts in place of the walnuts, if you like.

1 cup walnut pieces

¾ cup plus 2 tablespoons mayonnaise

1 to 2 lemons (see Box)

4 cups medium shreds roast chicken★

3 celery stalks, cut in half lengthwise and thinly sliced crosswise, plus 1 cup celery leaves from the inner heart of the bunch

1½ cups seedless red grapes, halved

½ cup thinly sliced fresh basil leaves

2 large scallions or 3 small ones, trimmed and thinly sliced crosswise

3 tablespoons coarsely chopped fresh tarragon leaves

1 tablespoon freshly ground coarse black pepper, or to taste, if you prefer a finer grind

1½ teaspoons flaky coarse sea salt, or to taste, if you have a finer salt

★From 1 (3½- to 4-pound) bird

Preheat the oven to 350°F with the rack in the middle. Spread the nuts on a baking sheet and bake until fragrant and lightly toasted, 8 to 12 minutes. Let the nuts cool, then coarsely chop.

Finely zest the lemon into a large bowl, holding the zester close so that you capture the flavorful oil that sprays from the lemon as you zest. Stir in the mayonnaise and 4 tablespoons lemon juice. Add the nuts and the remaining ingredients. Stir to combine well.

---

easy zesting and juicing

With the help of a simple hand held citrus reamer or press, you can get 4 tablespoons juice from 1 large lemon. If the lemons at the market are on the small to medium size, buy 2, use the zest from both lemons, then measure the juice. Handheld Microplane zesters are inexpensive and the quickest and easiest way to zest citrus. They're also terrific for grating cheeses, nutmeg, and more.

ROAST CHICKEN SALAD *with* SMOKED PAPRIKA MAYO, SERRANO HAM, *and* OLIVES

A few of Spain's most treasured goodies—sweet-salty Serrano ham, smoky paprika, and mild, plump, pimiento-stuffed olives—make a heck of a roast chicken salad. Tasty alongside a few leaves of Bibb lettuce, lightly dressed with sherry vinegar and good Spanish olive oil, both the salad and the dressed greens are terrific as a sandwich, too, made with slices of crusty baguette or soft country bread.

Serves 4 to 6

2 large eggs

½ cup mayonnaise

2 tablespoons fresh lemon juice

½ teaspoon Pimentón de la Vera (see Sources and Credits, page 170)

¼ teaspoon fine sea salt

Freshly ground coarse black pepper

4 cups medium shreds roast chicken*

⅔ cup coarsely chopped green pitted Spanish olives, coarsely chopped (from about 25 olives)

2 ounces ⅛-inch thick Serrano ham slices, cut into 1-inch matchsticks

¼ cup Marcona almonds, coarsely chopped

Flaky coarse sea salt

1 head Bibb lettuce, leaves separated

1½ tablespoons good-quality extra-virgin olive oil, Spanish if you like (see Sources and Credits, page 170)

1½ tablespoons sherry vinegar

*From 1 (3½- to 4-pound) bird

Bring a medium saucepan of water to a boil. Gently lower the eggs into the water and cook for 9 minutes, then drain and run under cold water until cool enough to handle. Peel the eggs and set them aside.

In a large bowl, whisk together the mayonnaise, lemon juice, Pimentón de la Vera, fine salt, and generous pinch of pepper, making sure that any clumps of Pimentón de la Vera are blended into the mixture. Add the chicken, olives, ham, and almonds; stir to combine. Adjust the salt and pepper to taste. Transfer the salad to a serving bowl or platter.

Slice the eggs crosswise, then place the egg slices on top of the chicken salad and sprinkle with coarse salt and pepper.

In a second large bowl, toss together the lettuce, oil, vinegar, and a generous pinch of coarse salt and pepper. Serve the chicken salad with the greens.

CURRIED CHICKEN SALAD *with* GOLDEN RAISINS, LIME, *and* HONEY

Serves 4

Raisins, lime, and honey create a sweet-tangy chutney flavor that plays nicely with the curry in this Indian-inspired salad. Whether under a tree in the park or around the table in cooler months, I love to serve this dish picnic-style, with good crackers and little gourmet bites from a cheese shop or olive bar. It's also tasty stuffed into a whole-wheat pita, or rolled up in crisp lettuce leaves.

1 tablespoon extra-virgin olive oil

1 medium yellow onion, finely chopped

1 tablespoon finely chopped ginger

1 tablespoon finely chopped garlic

1 tablespoon curry powder

1½ teaspoons fine sea salt

1 teaspoon ground cumin

4 cups small shreds roast chicken*

4½ tablespoons mayonnaise

3½ tablespoons plain yogurt

2 tablespoons fresh lime juice

2 teaspoons mild floral honey, like orange blossom

¼ cup plus 1 tablespoon golden raisins

1 box good-quality crackers

Gourmet bites (see Box)

*From 1 (3½- to 4-pound) bird

Heat the oil in a 12-inch skillet over medium heat. Add the onion, ginger, and garlic, and reduce the heat to low. Cook, stirring occasionally, until softened, about 10 minutes. Add the curry, salt, and cumin; stir to combine and cook 1 minute more. Add the chicken and stir to combine.

Transfer to a large bowl and let cool for a few minutes, then add the mayonnaise, yogurt, lime juice, and honey; stir to thoroughly combine.

Stir in the raisins. Serve with the crackers and gourmet bites.

---

a simple hunt for gourmet bites

Good cheese shops and supermarket olive bars are filled with treasures (sold by the pound or jarred) that can be quickly partnered with a simple chicken salad to create an impressive picnic spread. Look for crackers studded with dried olives or flavorful seeds, like fennel or caraway; stuffed grape leaves; roasted red peppers or sweet-hot peppadews; your favorite olives; and a mix of sweet or spicy pickled okra, green beans, carrots, and beets, and a few cornichons, or kosher dills.

FRISÉE SALAD *with* ROAST CHICKEN, FRESH FIGS, *and* SMOKED ALMONDS

Serves 4

I go a little fig-crazy when the plump delicate fruit pops into markets in late spring and then once again in late summer. Inspired by the classic figs with prosciutto, my mind made a natural leap to the pairing of the fruit with smoked almonds, which lend a touch of meaty flavor. Any variety of fig, or a mix, works well in this salad.

3 tablespoons finely chopped shallot (1 large)

2½ tablespoons sherry vinegar

Flaky coarse sea salt

5 tablespoons extra-virgin olive oil

1 head frisée (about ½ pound), torn into pieces

1½ cups medium to large shreds roast chicken

8 fresh purple and/or green figs, stemmed and cut into halves or quarters

Freshly ground black pepper

¼ cup coarsely chopped smoked almonds

In a large bowl, combine the shallot, vinegar, and ½ teaspoon salt. Let stand for 15 minutes.

In a slow and steady stream, add the oil to the shallot mixture, whisking all the while, to combine.

Add the frisée, chicken, and a generous pinch of salt to the bowl with the dressing, and toss to combine. Arrange the frisée and chicken on individual plates (reserve the bowl).

Add the figs to the dressing bowl with a generous pinch of salt and pepper, and gently toss to coat with any dressing that's left behind. Arrange the figs on the plates and sprinkle the salads with the almonds and a pinch of salt.

CHICORY SALAD *with* ROAST CHICKEN, CRISPY CROUTONS, *and* TOASTED GARLIC VINAIGRETTE

Serves 4

Chicory, with its twisty, pleasingly bitter leaves, is also called curly endive. Frisée, a similar lettuce, with straighter and wispier leaves, can be substituted. The technique of toasting the garlic in warm olive oil for the vinaigrette is easy. Just be sure to keep the heat low and lift up the pan as necessary to keep the oil from becoming too hot, so the garlic slowly cooks through and does not burn.

½ cup extra-virgin olive oil

1½ cups cubed (¼-inch) rustic bread (about 1½ ounces)

4 garlic cloves, finely chopped

½ teaspoon fine sea salt

1½ tablespoons white wine vinegar

½ pound chicory (1 head French curly endive) or frisée, tough outer leaves discarded and remaining leaves torn into 2-inch pieces

1½ cups medium shreds roast chicken

½ teaspoon flaky coarse sea salt

½ teaspoon freshly ground black pepper

Heat the oil and 1 bread cube in a small skillet over medium-high heat until the bread turns golden. Remove the test cube, add the remaining cubes, and fry, carefully stirring with a slotted spoon, until golden, about 30 seconds. Transfer the croutons to paper towels to drain. Strain the oil through a fine-mesh sieve and reserve.

In a small saucepan or skillet, combine the reserved oil and the garlic and cook over low heat until the oil begins to bubble. Continue cooking, picking up the skillet to swirl the pan and give it a break from the heat, every 10 seconds or so, until the garlic is lightly golden and tender (you can test it with the tip of a paring knife), about 9 minutes. Remove the skillet from the heat, and, using a slotted spoon, transfer the garlic to a plate to cool (reserve the oil).

Use the side of your knife and the blade to alternately mash and gently scrape the toasted garlic and the fine salt together, until you have a garlic paste. Transfer the paste to a large bowl, add the vinegar, and whisk to combine. In a slow and steady stream, whisk in the reserved oil.

Add the chicory, chicken, and croutons to the bowl; toss to combine. Season with the coarse salt and pepper.

TABBOULEH *with* ROAST CHICKEN

Homemade tabbouleh, especially when heavy on the lemon and herbs, has an extraordinarily fresh and vibrant quality that is lacking in most store-bought versions. Though the bulgur requires some time to soak, by the time you're finished chopping up the herbs and vegetables, the salad is tossed together in minutes. Adding chicken makes this dish a little heartier than the vegetarian type. Serve it on its own, or mezze-style, with olives and other little salads and bites.

Serves 4

¾ cup fine bulgur

½ cup fresh lemon juice

1¾ cups thinly sliced roast chicken

1 medium cucumber, peeled and cut into ⅛-inch dice

4 medium or 5 small radishes, thinly sliced

1¼ cups finely chopped fresh mint leaves

¾ cup finely chopped fresh flat-leaf parsley leaves

3 to 4 scallions, trimmed and thinly sliced

⅓ cup extra-virgin olive oil

Flaky coarse sea salt

Freshly ground black pepper

Combine the bulgur and lemon juice in a large bowl and let stand for 45 minutes.

Fluff the mixture with a fork, then add the chicken, cucumber, radishes, mint, parsley, scallions, and oil. Stir to thoroughly combine. Season with salt and pepper.

a fine grind

Bulgur comes in fine, medium, and coarse grinds. The fine grind works best for this recipe. If it's not available, purchase the medium or coarse, and pulse it a few times in a spice grinder or food processor to make it fine.

CHICKEN and RICE SALAD with MINT PESTO and PEAS

Serves 4

This is a great salad for a summer picnic or to bring to the beach. It also works well in those last weeks of winter, when you want to summon the warm breezes of spring.

1½ cups frozen peas, thawed

Good basic kitchen salt, like kosher (for water)

4 tablespoons extra-virgin olive oil

1 teaspoon fine sea salt

1 cup long-grain white rice

2 cups packed fresh mint leaves, plus a small handful of leaves for garnish

1 cup fresh basil leaves

½ cup freshly grated Parmigiano-Reggiano cheese (about 2 ounces)

¼ cup pine nuts

¼ cup fresh lemon juice

1 garlic clove, peeled

1½ cups small to medium shreds roast chicken

1 small cucumber, peeled, seeded, and cut into ¼-inch cubes

3 scallions, trimmed and thinly sliced on a long diagonal

Bring a small saucepan of well-salted water to a boil. Add the peas and cook until tender, about 2 minutes. Drain and set aside.

Bring 1¾ cups water, 1 tablespoon oil, and ½ teaspoon fine salt to a boil in a 2-quart saucepan, then stir in rice. Return to a boil and cover. Reduce heat to low and simmer the rice until the water is absorbed and rice is tender, about 15 minutes. Fluff rice with a fork and let stand, covered, 5 minutes. Spread the rice on a baking sheet and let cool to room temperature.

In a food processor, combine ½ cup of the cooked peas, 2 cups mint, basil, cheese, pine nuts, lemon juice, garlic, and remaining ½ teaspoon fine salt. Purée until smooth.

In a bowl, toss together the cooked rice, remaining 1 cup cooked peas, pesto, chicken, cucumber, and about ⅔ of the scallions. Transfer to a serving bowl and sprinkle with the remaining scallions and handful of mint leaves.

HARICOTS VERTS *with* ROAST CHICKEN, CARAMELIZED ONIONS, *and* CRÈME FRAÎCHE

Crème fraîche, an unctuous, slightly tangy thickened cream, and sweet caramelized onions add indulgence to the act of "eating your green beans." I am partial to haricots verts—the slender, French-style green beans—but any string bean can be used here. String beans, like many other vegetables, are sweetest when freshly picked, so buy them fresh and local whenever you can.

Serves 4

Good basic kitchen salt, like kosher (for water)

1½ tablespoons extra-virgin olive oil

½ tablespoon unsalted butter

¾ pound Spanish or yellow onions, halved lengthwise, peeled, and cut into ¼-inch slices

Flaky coarse sea salt

Freshly ground black pepper

¼ cup pine nuts

1 pound haricots verts, or other skinny green beans, trimmed

1½ cups large shreds roast chicken

5 tablespoons crème fraîche

Bring a large saucepan of well-salted water to a boil.

Heat the oil and butter in a 12-inch heavy skillet over medium-high heat. Add the onions and a pinch of salt and pepper and cook, stirring occasionally and reducing the heat every 10 minutes or so, until the onions are caramelized, 40 to 45 minutes.

Meanwhile, in a small skillet, heat the pine nuts over low heat, shaking the pan back and forth frequently, until the nuts are golden, 10 to 12 minutes.

Add the beans to the boiling water and cook, partially covered, until just tender, about 7 minutes. Drain in a colander, then run under cold water until cooled, drain, pat dry well, and transfer to a large bowl. Add the chicken, crème fraîche, ⅔ of the onions, and pine nuts and toss to combine. Using your fingers, crush enough coarse salt to make about ¾ teaspoon, add to the salad with a generous sprinkle of pepper, and toss once more.

Transfer to a serving plate, scatter the remaining onions over the top, and add a second sprinkle of coarse salt and pepper to taste.

with or without the chicken

Try this salad, sans bird, as a Thanksgiving side (it can easily be scaled up for a large crowd), then, if you have any leftover salad, you can add shreds of turkey (in place of chicken) for delicious "day-after" fare.

MIDDLE EASTERN ROAST CHICKEN *and* BREAD SALAD

Serves 4

This is *fattoush*—a lively, herby, and lemony Lebanese salad. The technique of mashing raw garlic and salt together to form a paste serves several purposes: The salt seasons and mellows the bite of the raw cloves, and the mashing turns the duo into a paste that can be nicely emulsified into a salad dressing. Sumac, the ground dried berries of a sumac tree, offers a tangy flavor and beautiful color. It's a nice, albeit optional, finishing touch.

1 garlic clove, finely chopped

Fine sea salt

½ cup fresh lemon juice

3 (4- to 5-inch) pita breads, toasted and torn into small pieces

½ pound romaine lettuce hearts, leaves separated and torn

1¾ cups shredded roast chicken

1 medium cucumber, peeled, halved lengthwise, and thinly sliced on the bias

1 cup finely chopped fresh mint leaves

½ cup finely chopped fresh flat-leaf parsley leaves

3 scallions, trimmed and thinly sliced

¼ cup plus 2 tablespoons extra-virgin olive oil

Flaky coarse sea salt

Freshly ground black pepper

Sumac, optional (see Sources and Credits, page 170)

Use the side of your knife and the blade to alternately chop and gently scrape the garlic and ¾ teaspoon fine salt together, until you have a garlic paste. Scrape the paste into a large serving bowl, add the lemon juice, and whisk together.

Add the pita, lettuce, chicken, cucumber, mint, parsley, and scallions to the bowl. Drizzle with the oil and toss well to combine. Season with coarse salt, pepper, and sumac, if using, and serve immediately.

---

garlic know-how

Garlic is best (juicy and full-flavored) when it is fresh, local, and in season (from early summer into fall). Buy it freshly harvested from a local grower whenever you can. Stored garlic, which is what we all buy in the winter months, becomes aggressive in flavor, and the cloves develop a green shoot in the center. Cut the cloves in half and pull out and discard the shoot to minimize bitterness and pungency.

SOBA NOODLE SALAD *with* ROAST CHICKEN, CUCUMBER, PEANUTS, *and* MINT

Serves 4 to 6

Soba noodles come in many varieties; you'll find some made with 100 percent buckwheat and others with lotus root, mugwort, wild yam, and more. I'm partial to the 100 percent buckwheat, which has a rich, earthy flavor. You can use whichever you like best, just be sure to cook soba "al dente" (using a pasta-cooking method), or prepare them Japanese-style, by bringing a pot of water to a boil, adding the noodles, and stirring well (to prevent sticking). When the water returns to the boil, "shock" it by adding ½ to ⅔ cup cold water, then repeat the process 4 or 5 times, or until the noodles are cooked through but still firm. This is an easygoing salad with clean, cooling flavors.

1 pound dried soba noodles

1 large cucumber

3 tablespoons Asian sesame oil

1¼ teaspoons fine sea salt

2 cups small shreds roast chicken

2 scallions, trimmed and thinly sliced

½ cup coarsely chopped fresh mint leaves

⅓ cup coarsely chopped roasted salted peanuts

Shichimi togarashi, *ichimi togarashi*, Aleppo pepper, or red pepper flakes, optional

Bring a large pot of unsalted water to a boil. Add the noodles and cook according to package directions, stirring occasionally, until tender.

Meanwhile, cut the cucumber in half lengthwise, then seed and cut crosswise into thin slices.

Drain the noodles in a colander and rinse with cold water. Transfer to a large bowl. Add the sesame oil and toss to coat, then add the salt and toss again. Add the cucumber, chicken, scallions, mint, and peanuts. Toss to thoroughly combine. Adjust the seasoning, if necessary. Sprinkle with *schichimi togarashi* or other chile pepper, if you like a little heat.

hot stuff

Shichimi togarashi and *ichimi togarashi* are flavorful Japanese spices that you can use to add heat to this or any other dish. *Shichimi* is ground red chile pepper, flecked with mandarin orange peel, sesame seeds, nori, and other flavorings, while *ichimi* is unflavored ground chile (*ichi* meaning one, for "one flavor"). You'll find these spices in Asian markets and online. More basic red pepper flakes can be substituted.

WARM CHICKEN *and* BARLEY SALAD *with* SKILLET MUSHROOMS, GARLIC, *and* HERBS

Toothsome barley with fresh herbs and earthy mushrooms makes a very satisfying, healthy salad. Resist fussing with the mushrooms once they are added to the skillet so that they brown up well, with nice crisped-up edges.

Serves 4

Flaky coarse sea salt

¾ cup pearled barley

¼ cup plus 3½ tablespoons extra-virgin olive oil

½ pound shiitake mushrooms, stems trimmed, caps cut in half, if large

½ pound button mushrooms, stems trimmed, mushrooms halved or quartered, if large

1 garlic clove, finely chopped

1½ cups large shreds roast chicken

Freshly ground black pepper

⅓ cup finely chopped fresh flat-leaf parsley leaves

2 tablespoons finely chopped fresh chives

2 tablespoons finely chopped fresh mint leaves

4 ounces arugula, tough stems removed

1 tablespoon red wine vinegar

1 lemon, quartered

Bring 8 cups water and 1 teaspoon coarse salt to a boil in a large saucepan. Add the barley. Once the water returns to a boil, reduce to a low boil and cook until tender yet still firm to the bite, 40 to 45 minutes.

About 20 minutes before the barley is ready, cook the mushrooms. Heat ¼ cup oil in a 12-inch heavy nonstick skillet over medium-high heat. Add about ⅓ of the mushrooms and stir once or twice, then cook without stirring, until mushrooms begin to brown, about 3 minutes. Push the mushrooms to the side of the pan and add more mushrooms in the same manner, until all of the mushrooms are in the skillet and nicely browned, about 10 minutes total (if, toward the end, the first handful is browning too much, push them on top). Remove the skillet from the heat. Add the garlic, then the chicken and toss to combine thoroughly. Season with salt and pepper.

Drain the cooked barley and transfer to a large bowl; add 2 tablespoons of the remaining oil, the parsley, chives, and mint. Then add the mushroom mixture and stir to combine. Season with 1 teaspoon salt and ¼ teaspoon pepper.

In a second bowl, toss the arugula with the remaining 1½ tablespoons oil and the vinegar. Season to taste with salt and pepper. Serve the arugula alongside the warm barley and mushrooms, with a squeeze of lemon over the top.

Chapter four

ROAST CHICKEN SOUPS

ROAST CHICKEN BROTH

Makes about 2 to 3 quarts

There's no match—in quality or flavor—for homemade broth. It's peerless for making soups, risottos, and more; the perfect tonic when you're feeling under the weather; or a satisfying midday snack, sipped from a mug on a chilly day. To make broth, you're using ingredients you might otherwise throw away: a picked-over roast chicken carcass; an odd carrot, celery stalk, or onion; a stray herb sprig or two. These are the basics, but making broth is an improvisational endeavor. If you like, add a chunk or two of peeled celery root, a coarsely chopped parsnip, a piece of Parmigiano-Reggiano cheese rind, mushroom stems, a halved tomato or two, and/or a couple of whole dried chiles. The longer it slowly simmers, the richer the broth becomes—make a light or rich brew; it's up to you. A rich broth can always be stretched with a little water if you don't have enough for a recipe.

1 or 2 roast chicken carcasses, picked of meat, plus necks, if you have them

1 medium yellow onion, quartered (with skin on)

2 to 4 gently smashed garlic cloves with peel, or 1 whole head of garlic, with the top ½ inch cut off to expose the cloves, if making a larger batch of broth

1 to 2 large carrots, washed and cut into 2-inch pieces

1 to 2 stalks celery, washed and cut into 2-inch pieces

1 teaspoon whole black peppercorns

A handful of fresh parsley sprigs, and/or other savory fresh herb sprigs, such as rosemary, oregano, marjoram, sage, and thyme

Combine all of the ingredients, and as many of the optional ingredients (see Headnote) as you like in a large pot and add water to cover by several inches. Bring the water to a simmer over medium heat, then reduce the heat so that you have a bare simmer (bubbles just breaking the surface of the water), and cook until the broth is reduced and flavorful. This will generally take 2 to 3 hours for a light broth, or 3 to 6 hours for a richer broth.

When the broth is ready, pour it through a fine-mesh sieve into a large bowl and discard the solids. If using the broth right away, skim off and discard any fat. If not, cool the broth completely, then chill, covered, and discard any solidified fat. When you go to use the broth, you can season it to taste with salt. Broth can be chilled for 3 days or frozen for 1 month.

using the freezer for roast chicken broth

As you roast chickens, freeze necks, backs, and carcasses in resealable bags. Fresh herbs and Parmesan rinds can also be kept frozen for use in broths. Ingredients do not need to be defrosted before using. You can make a broth with just one carcass, or wait until you have two or more for a larger batch. Once made, freeze broth in 2- to 4-cup plastic containers, depending on how you use it. Leave 1 inch of space between the broth and the lid; liquid expands when it freezes. Label and date frozen broth, and use it within six to eight months.

ROAST CHICKEN SOUP *with* WHEAT BERRIES, PARSNIPS, *and* KALE

Serves 4

The chewy bite of hearty wheat berries is nice in soups. The grain is easy to cook and soaks up the flavor of a good—especially homemade—chicken broth. Try mustard greens or turnip tops in place of the kale, if you like. When you want a more complex dish and a little richness and protein, top this soup with a poached egg.

8 cups chicken broth, preferably homemade (page 100)

¾ cup wheat berries or spelt

¾ pound parsnips (about 2 medium), peeled, quartered lengthwise, cores cut out if woody

½ pound kale

1 cup medium shreds roast chicken

Flaky coarse sea salt

Freshly ground black pepper

¼ lemon, cut in half

Good-quality extra-virgin olive oil for drizzling

Combine the broth and wheat berries in a large saucepan. Bring to a boil over high heat. Reduce to a simmer and cook, covered, until the wheat berries are tender and chewy, about 1 hour.

Meanwhile, cut the parsnips into ⅓-inch cubes. Cut the center ribs from the kale and discard. Cut the leaves crosswise into 1-inch slices.

When the wheat berries are tender, stir in the parsnips, kale, and chicken, and simmer until the vegetables are just tender, 3 to 5 minutes. Season the soup with salt and pepper (if you are using unsalted homemade broth, you may need to season generously with salt).

Ladle the soup into bowls, squeeze a little lemon juice over the top of each serving, and drizzle with oil.

cooking healthy grains does not have to slow you down

Getting food to the table quickly is often more about good kitchen organization than anything else. Wheat berries require about 1 hour cooking time. Set up your simmering broth and grains first. While the grains are cooking, prepare the parsnips and kale. By the time you set the table and tidy up the kitchen, the soup will be ready for its quick final steps. You can also cook the wheat berries in the broth 1 to 2 days ahead, and then finish preparing the soup in about 15 minutes, just before serving.

ROAST CHICKEN SOUP
with POTATOES *and* FENNEL

Serves 4

One chilly February afternoon, my husband Steve and I pulled some chicken, fennel, and leftover roasted potatoes from the fridge, and, in minutes, put together this soup, which is now one of our favorites. If you don't already have potatoes roasted, your soup will take a bit longer to cook, but not much. The spuds are cut small, so they cook up quickly. I have tried using boiled potatoes here, but the flavor and the starchy quality of the roasted is much better.

¾ **pound fingerling or other small heirloom potatoes**

1 tablespoon extra-virgin olive oil

Flaky coarse sea salt

4 cups chicken broth, preferably homemade (page 100)

1 small fennel bulb, cored and cut into ¼-inch pieces, fronds roughly chopped

1½ cups medium shreds roasted chicken

Freshly ground black pepper

Preheat the oven to 425°F with the rack in the middle. Line a baking sheet with parchment paper.

Cut the potatoes in half lengthwise, then cut the pieces into halves or quarters, depending on their size. On the prepared baking sheet, toss the potatoes with the oil and ¼ teaspoon salt. Roast for 15 minutes, then toss and stir. Continue roasting until tender, about 5 minutes more. Remove the potatoes from the oven and transfer to a cutting board; let sit until cool enough to handle, then cut into bite-size pieces.

Bring the broth to a simmer in a large saucepan. Add the fennel pieces, return the broth to a simmer and cook for 1 minute, then add the potatoes and chicken. Continue to cook the soup until the fennel is just tender, about 2 minutes more.

Remove the soup from the heat and season with salt and pepper. Ladle into bowls and top with the fennel fronds.

ROAST CHICKEN NOODLE SOUP
with LEEKS, PEAS, and DILL

Rings of lightly caramelized leeks give an otherwise simple chicken noodle soup a buttery sweetness and visual elegance. Purchase long, skinny leeks rather than the squatter, fatter types, if you have a choice (you'll get more rings), or buy an extra leek. You can use any shape small noodle or break up larger ones, like pappardelle, to make square-like pieces.

Serves 4 to 6

2 tablespoons extra-virgin olive oil

3 leeks, tough outer leaves discarded, white and very pale green parts cut crosswise into ⅓-inch pieces, keeping rings intact

Flaky coarse sea salt

Freshly ground black pepper

7 cups chicken broth, preferably homemade (page 100)

1 garlic clove, gently smashed and peeled

6 ounces small noodles (see Headnote)

3 cups medium shreds roast chicken

2 cups frozen peas, thawed

2 tablespoons finely chopped fresh dill leaves

Heat the oil in a 12-inch skillet over medium-high heat. Add the leeks in a single layer. Reduce the heat to medium-low, season the leeks with a generous pinch of salt and pepper, and cook, turning once and reducing heat to low midway through, until both sides are golden, about 18 minutes.

Meanwhile, bring the broth and garlic to a boil in a 5-quart pot, stir in the noodles and cook, stirring occasionally, until tender but still firm to the bite, 10 to 12 minutes. Remove and discard the garlic.

Set aside a few leeks per serving for garnish. Add the remaining leeks to the soup, along with the chicken, peas, and dill and cook for 2 minutes more. Season with salt and pepper. Ladle into bowls and garnish with the reserved leeks.

LENTIL SOUP *with* ROAST CHICKEN, SWISS CHARD, *and* PARMIGIANO-REGGIANO CHEESE

Serves 6

The shards of Parmigiano-Reggiano that garnish this soup are much more than mere embellishment. The nutty, spicy, salty qualities of the cheese perk up the earthy nature of the lentils and pull together the rest of the flavors in the soup. Look for French or Spanish pardina, or Italian castellucio or colfiorito (both from Umbria), when buying your lentils. These types cook until tender with a rich flavor and a toothsome, not mushy, bite.

3 tablespoons extra-virgin olive oil

1 medium yellow onion, finely chopped

1 medium carrot, finely chopped

1 celery stalk, finely chopped

3 garlic cloves, gently smashed and peeled

1½ cups lentils (see Headnote), sorted of debris and rinsed

4 cups chicken broth, preferably homemade (page 100)

2½ tablespoons tomato paste

1 cup Parmigiano-Reggiano cheese, cut into shards (4½ to 5 ounces), plus rind (rind optional)

¾ to 1 pound red Swiss chard

2 cups small shreds roast chicken

2 to 3 tablespoons fresh lemon juice

Fine sea salt

Freshly ground black pepper

In a 5- to 6-quart heavy pot or Dutch oven, heat the oil over medium heat. Add the onion and carrot, reduce the heat to medium-low, and cook until softened, about 10 minutes. Add the celery and garlic cloves and cook, stirring occasionally, 2 to 3 minutes more, then stir in the lentils. Add the broth, 1½ cups of water, tomato paste, and Parmesan rind (reserve the shards), if using; increase the heat to medium–high, and bring to a boil, then reduce to a gentle simmer and cook, stirring occasionally, until the lentils are tender yet still firm to the bite, 40 to 45 minutes.

While the lentils are cooking, cut the stems and center ribs from the Swiss chard, discarding any tough portions, then cut the stems and ribs crosswise into ½-inch pieces. Coarsely chop the leaves. When the lentils are tender, stir in the chard and chicken, return soup to a simmer, and cook for 5 minutes. Remove and discard the Parmesan rind. Add the lemon juice and ¾ teaspoon salt, then adjust the salt and pepper to taste. Serve hot, with the Parmesan shards sprinkled on top.

MEXICAN CHICKEN SOUP *with* RICE

No fancy flourishes here. This is, simply put, a delicious and satisfying, light soup. Save some of the jalapeño seeds, either to sprinkle into the soup as it cooks or over the top when serving, if you like extra spice. A dash or two of hot sauce can also be used.

2 garlic cloves, finely chopped

Fine sea salt

2 quarts chicken broth, preferably homemade (page 100)

½ cup long-grain white rice

1 small white onion, cut into ¼-inch dice

1 large jalapeño chile, cut in half, seeded, and cut into ¼-inch dice (seeds can be reserved and added to the soup, if you like it spicy)

1½ cups small shreds roast chicken

2 medium tomatoes, cored and cut into ¼-inch dice

2 tablespoons coarsely chopped fresh cilantro leaves, plus whole sprigs for garnish

1 firm-ripe avocado, pitted and sliced

2 scallions, trimmed and thinly sliced on a long diagonal

1 lime, quartered

Use the side of your knife and the blade to alternately chop and gently scrape the garlic and a generous ⅛ teaspoon salt together, until you have a garlic paste. Put the garlic paste and the broth into a 5- to 6-quart heavy pot and bring to a simmer, then add the rice and simmer for 10 minutes.

Add the onion and jalapeño, and continue to simmer the soup until the rice is tender, about 10 minutes more. Add the chicken, tomatoes, and chopped cilantro, and cook for 1 minute more, then season with salt.

Ladle the soup into bowls and top with the cilantro sprigs, avocado, scallions, and a good squeeze of lime juice.

LEMON CHICKEN SOUP *with* RICE (AVGOLEMONO)

Serves 4

This classic Greek soup is one of my longtime favorites and a must for lemon lovers. Light, yet satisfyingly rich, its flavor is a balanced blend of salty citrus tang. Short-grain rice—starchier than long-grain types—thickens the soup and adds to its creamy quality.

6 cups chicken broth, preferably homemade (see page 100)

⅓ cup Arborio or other short-grain rice

3 large eggs

½ cup fresh lemon juice

Flaky coarse sea salt

Freshly ground black pepper

¾ cup small shreds roast chicken, at room temperature

Coarsely chopped fresh dill, fennel fronds, or parsley for garnish (optional)

Bring the broth to a boil in a 5-quart heavy pot, stir in the rice and cook, covered, at a gentle simmer, until the rice is tender, about 15 minutes. Remove from the heat and cover to keep warm.

In a medium bowl, beat the eggs, then beat in the lemon juice a little at a time, whisking constantly, to thoroughly combine. Slowly add about ¼ cup of the broth, whisking vigorously. Repeat twice, then add the egg mixture back into the pot with the broth, whisking to combine. Season with salt and pepper to taste. Add the chicken, ladle into bowls, and garnish with dill, fennel fronds, or parsley, if you like.

Note: If you are serving the soup later, warm it very gently over low heat in lieu of simmering or boiling, which can cause the eggs to coagulate and the soup to become stringy.

> *to soften the tang (only if desired)...*
>
> *Avgolemono* means "egg-lemon" in Greek, referring to the two key ingredients of its namesake soup. The intensity of the lemon softens over time, which some may prefer, and you can make this soup a day or two ahead, if you wish, or use a little less lemon. When reheating, do so gently over low heat, to keep the texture of the soup smooth.

BLACK BEAN *and* ANCHO CHILE SOUP *with* ROASTED CHICKEN, CILANTRO, *and* LIME

Serves 4 to 6

When I was five years old, my dad accepted an opportunity to spend six months or so working on an advertising account in Mexico City. The whole family immediately fell in love with the vibrant culture and exotic new tastes of our temporary home. Mom learned to cook on a *comal*, the smooth, flat all-purpose griddle that is used to toast chiles, sear meats, and make tortillas. To this day, toasting the chiles to make this soup brings me back to that exciting time, though at home in New York, I use a cast-iron skillet for the job (a stainless-steel skillet works fine, too). Adding a generous squeeze of fresh lime juice to the dish just before serving is a must. The acid brightens up and pulls together all of the rich flavors within.

1 pound dried black beans, soaked for 8 hours or overnight, and drained

4½ cups chicken broth, preferably homemade (page 100)

1 ounce dried ancho chiles (about 4)

1¼ cups finely chopped white onion

3 garlic cloves, gently smashed and peeled

1 teaspoon dried oregano

Fine sea salt

1½ cups medium shreds roast chicken

1½ ounces fully cooked Mexican or Spanish chorizo, very thinly sliced (optional)

2 teaspoons extra-virgin olive oil (optional)

4 to 6 lime wedges (from 1 to 2 limes)

Fresh cilantro leaves for garnish

1 firm-ripe avocado, pitted and cubed

In a 5- to 6-quart heavy pot or Dutch oven, combine the beans, broth, and 2½ cups water. Bring to a gentle simmer and cook, partially covered, for 1 hour, adding water, if necessary, to keep the beans just covered.

Meanwhile, remove the stems from the chiles and discard. Using a knife or kitchen shears, slit the chiles down the side then flatten them out as much as possible. Discard the seeds.

Warm a skillet over medium heat (don't let the pan get too hot, or the chiles will burn and turn bitter). Lightly toast the chiles by pressing them, inside down, on the warmed pan for 3 seconds; turn over and press until the inside flesh turns brown, about 3 seconds more. Submerge the chiles in a bowl of hot tap water, stirring occasionally, for 30 minutes.

Drain the chiles, reserving the soaking water. In a blender, purée the chiles with 3 tablespoons of the soaking liquid until thick and smooth. Stir the chile purée, onion, garlic, and oregano into the beans, crumbling the oregano between your fingers as you add it to release more of the flavor. Add water to just cover the beans by a ½ inch or so. Continue cooking, partially covered, stirring occasionally and adding water, if necessary, to keep beans just covered, until the beans are very tender, 30 to 45 minutes more.

(see following page)

Remove and discard the garlic cloves from the soup, then stir in 1½ teaspoons salt. Transfer 1½ cups of the soup to a blender and purée until smooth. Add the puréed soup back to the pot, add the chicken, and stir to combine. Adjust the salt to taste.

If using chorizo, heat in a skillet with oil over medium-high heat, stirring occasionally, until browned, about 1 to 2 minutes.

Rewarm the soup and ladle into bowls. Squeeze lime over each serving and garnish with the chorizo, cilantro, and avocado.

GALICIAN-INSPIRED BEANS, GREENS, and ROAST CHICKEN SOUP

Serves 4

My dear friend, Alex Raij (a gem of a chef, who, with her equally talented husband, Eder Montero, owns two of New York City's most exciting restaurants, Txikito and El Quinto Pino) taught me how to make Cocido Madrileño, a tender pork and chickpea stew from Madrid. Making the stew is magical. Soaked chickpeas, a hunk of slab bacon, chicken thighs, and a meaty ham hock are combined in a pot with aromatics and water, and slowly simmered. Before long, you have a rich, meaty dish that needs nothing more than a drizzle of good olive oil and some crusty country bread for sopping. This version, similar but Galician in style, shares the unfussy technique and is equally delicious.

1½ cups dried white beans, such as great Northern, navy, or cannellini (about 10 ounces)

1 head garlic, unpeeled

½ teaspoon dried thyme

4-ounce piece fully cooked Mexican or Spanish chorizo

3-ounce end piece speck, Serrano ham, or prosciutto, cut into 4 pieces

1 medium carrot, peeled and cut crosswise into 3 pieces

1 small unpeeled yellow onion

¾ pound kale

1½ cups medium shreds roast chicken

Fine sea salt

Good-quality extra-virgin olive oil

Flaky coarse sea salt

Freshly ground black pepper

Rustic bread for sopping

In a wide 5½- to 7-quart heavy pot, combine 3 quarts water, beans, garlic, and thyme. Soak for 8 hours, or overnight.

Add the chorizo, speck, carrot, and onion to the pot and place over medium heat. Bring the liquid to a simmer and cook, partially covered, until the beans are tender, 50 minutes or more (see Box on page 64).

Meanwhile, cut the center ribs from the kale and discard. Cut the leaves crosswise into 1-inch strips.

Using a slotted spoon, remove and discard the pieces of speck and the garlic. Remove the chorizo and set aside. Transfer the carrot pieces and the onion to a plate.

When cool enough to handle, peel the onion and combine in a blender with the carrot, ¾ cup of the beans, and ½ cup of the cooking liquid. Purée until smooth, then add the mixture back to the pot and stir to combine.

Thinly slice the chorizo. Add the kale, sliced chorizo, and chicken to the pot and stir to combine; stir in 1 teaspoon fine sea salt. Warm the soup over medium heat, stirring occasionally, until the kale is tender, about 5 minutes. Adjust the salt, if necessary.

Serve the soup with a drizzle of oil, a sprinkle of coarse salt and pepper, and some rustic bread for sopping.

CARROT SOUP *with* CHICKEN *and* THYME

Serves 4

A little bit of potato gives this soup its velvety-smooth texture. The carrots are slowly stewed, which coaxes out their sweetness. Pick up fresh-dug types at your farmers' market, whenever possible, for the most vibrant carrot taste.

2 tablespoons extra-virgin olive oil

1 tablespoon unsalted butter

1¾ cups coarsely chopped white onion

1½ pounds carrots, peeled and cut crosswise into ¼-inch slices

¼ pound new or Yukon gold potatoes, peeled and cut into ¼-inch cubes

Fine sea salt

4 cups chicken broth, preferably homemade (page 100)

Sugar (optional)

2 teaspoons white peppercorns

1 cup small shreds roast chicken, at room temperature

1½ teaspoons fresh thyme leaves

4 thin slices lemon

Heat the oil and butter in a 5½- to 7-quart Dutch oven or heavy saucepan with lid over medium heat until the butter is melted. Add the onion, reduce the heat to low, cover and cook until softened, about 15 minutes. Stir in the carrots, potatoes, and ½ teaspoon salt, and continue cooking, covered, for 10 minutes more.

Add the broth, increase the heat to medium, and bring to a simmer. Gently simmer, uncovered, until the vegetables are tender, 25 to 30 minutes. Carefully purée the soup in a blender until smooth, then return to the pot, gently reheat, and adjust the seasoning, adding a pinch or 2 of sugar to sweeten the soup if the carrots are not sweet enough.

In a mortar and pestle or, using the heel of your hand on the flat side of a chef's knife, coarsely crack the peppercorns. Divide the soup into serving bowls and top each serving with the chicken and thyme leaves. Squeeze a little lemon juice from slices into bowls of soup, then drop the slices into the bowls as a garnish. Sprinkle with the crushed peppercorns.

CHICKEN PHO

A homemade broth really shines here, and, though you can use a carcass from any bird to make it, consider the tea-brined chicken on page 41—for both the meat and to make the broth—since its flavors are so complementary. The chiles, bean sprouts, and other accompaniments are as much a part of this soup as the noodles, broth, and chicken. A good squeeze of fresh lime juice, which perks up and sharpens the flavors of the dish, is especially key.

1 medium sweet onion, such as Vidalia

1 (3-inch) piece fresh ginger, quartered and gently bruised with the flat side of a chef's knife

8 cups chicken broth, preferably homemade (page 100)

6 whole cloves

4 whole star anise pods

1 (3-inch) cinnamon stick

¾ pound rice stick noodles

¾ teaspoon Asian fish sauce (see Sources and Credits, page 170)

¼ teaspoon sugar

1½ to 2 cups small to medium shreds roast chicken

2 scallions, trimmed and thinly sliced on a long diagonal (optional)

1 or 2 Thai bird chiles (optional)

1 cup bean sprouts (optional)

4 lime wedges

Fresh mint, basil, or cilantro leaves, or a combination

Freshly ground black pepper

Hoisin sauce (see Sources and Credits, page 170)

Sriracha sauce (see Sources and Credits, page 170)

Crosswise, cut two ¼-inch slices from the onion; reserve the remaining onion. Working with one slice at a time, char the onion and ginger slices by using tongs to hold them over an open burner flame (alternatively, you can char them in a dry hot cast-iron skillet or on a grill pan).

In a large saucepan, combine the charred onion and ginger, broth, cloves, star anise, and cinnamon. Bring to a simmer over medium heat, then gently simmer until the broth is infused with spices, about 30 minutes. Meanwhile, in a shallow baking dish, soak the noodles in cold water for 30 minutes.

Remove the broth from the heat and stir in the fish sauce and sugar. Cover to keep warm.

Drain the noodles, then return them to the baking dish. Pour boiling water on top, and using tongs, gently agitate for 2 minutes, then drain and divide among four bowls. Top each with the chicken.

Gently reheat the broth, then ladle it over the chicken and noodles. Top with several or all of the following: paper-thin slices from the reserved onion, the scallions, chiles, and bean sprouts. Add a big squeeze of lime, the herbs, and black pepper. Pass the hoisin and Sriracha sauces at the table, inviting guests to add each to their liking.

THAI COCONUT SOUP *with* ROAST CHICKEN

If you're unfamiliar with lemongrass, galangal, Asian fish sauce, or coconut milk, rest assured, they are relatively easy to find and a cinch to use. Fresh ginger can be substituted for galangal. Both ginger or galangal plus lemongrass (found in supermarket produce sections) infuse the chicken broth to form the basis of this soup. Lime juice and fish sauce are added off the heat, just before serving, to keep their flavors vibrant and fresh.

Serves 4 to 6

1 fresh lemongrass stalk, trimmed and outer layers discarded

6 cups chicken broth, preferably homemade (page 100)

1 (3-inch) piece galangal or ginger, cut in half crosswise and quartered

¾ pound bok choy

1¼ cups medium shreds roast chicken, at room temperature

⅓ pound shiitake mushrooms, trimmed and caps quartered

1 (14-ounce) can unsweetened coconut milk (see Box)

¼ cup fresh lime juice

¼ cup Asian fish sauce

Chile-garlic sauce (see Sources and Credits, page 170)

Fresh cilantro sprigs and/or thinly sliced scallion for garnish (optional)

Cut the lemongrass in half lengthwise, then bruise the pieces with the side of a chef's knife. Combine the lemongrass, broth, and galangal in a 5- to 6-quart heavy pot. Bring to a simmer and cook until the broth is fragrant and infused with the spices, 15 to 20 minutes.

Meanwhile, trim the bottom ⅛ to ¼ inch of the bok choy and separate the leaves. Cut the green leaves from the white stems. Stack the leaves and cut crosswise into ¾-inch strips. Cut the stems into ¼-inch cubes. Divide the stems, leaves, chicken, and mushrooms among serving bowls.

When the broth is fragrant and infused with the spices, whisk in the coconut milk. Continue to simmer the soup for 15 minutes more.

Remove the pot from the heat and, using tongs or a slotted spoon, discard the lemongrass and galangal, then whisk in the lime juice and fish sauce. Ladle the soup over the chicken and vegetables and spoon ½ to ¾ teaspoon chile-garlic sauce into each bowl. Garnish with the cilantro sprigs and/or scallion, if desired. Pass around extra chile-garlic sauce at the table.

---

coconut milk

The coconut milk will likely be separated when you open the can; just scrape it all into the pot and whisk to combine.

CORDOBAN GAZPACHO *with* SHREDDED ROAST CHICKEN (SALMOREJO)

Serves 4

This thicker-than-average version of gazpacho comes from Andulucia, in the south of Spain, where it is known as *salmorejo*. Roast chicken, not one of the traditional embellishments, is a nice addition (especially with crisped-up salty skin) if you have some around. Gazpacho is best when tomatoes are at their peak. The flavors of this soup deepen over a few hours and, even more so after a day, so make it ahead when you can.

4 cups cubed (¾-inch) rustic bread, cut into cubes (about 5 ounces), plus more for crispy croutons, if desired (see Box)

2½ pounds ripe tomatoes

2 garlic cloves, coarsely chopped

½ teaspoon fine sea salt

¼ cup good-quality extra-virgin olive oil, plus more for drizzling

2 to 3 tablespoons good-quality Sherry vinegar

1 (⅛-inch-thick) slice Serrano ham or prosciutto, cut into short matchsticks

½ cup small shreds roast chicken, at room temperature

¼ cup seeded and diced cucumber

1 large egg, hard-boiled and finely grated, optional (see Box)

Bring a medium saucepan of water to a boil. Meanwhile, put the bread cubes and ½ cup water in a bowl and toss to combine. Let the mixture sit for 5 minutes, then squeeze all of the excess water from the bread. Discard the water.

Add the tomatoes to the boiling water and cook for 30 seconds. Drain, peel, quarter, and seed. Combine the tomatoes, half of the bread, the garlic, and salt in a blender and purée until smooth. Add the remaining bread and, with the machine running, add the oil in a slow and steady stream. Add 2 tablespoons vinegar and blend to combine. Adjust the vinegar and salt, if necessary. Chill the soup at least 3 hours or up to 1 day.

Serve drizzled with good-quality extra-virgin olive oil and topped with the Serrano ham, roast chicken, cucumber, and crispy croutons and/or hard-boiled egg, if desired.

---

a hard-boiled egg and crispy croutons

To hard-boil the egg for this dish, bring a medium saucepan of water to a boil, then lower the egg into the water and cook for 10 minutes. Drain and rinse under cold running water until cool enough to peel. Peel, pat dry with a paper towel, and finely grate into a bowl. The egg can be boiled 1 day ahead and grated up to 4 hours before serving. For crispy croutons, cut enough rustic bread into ¼-inch cubes to fill 1 cup. Heat ½ inch olive oil and 1 bread cube in a small skillet over medium-high heat until it turns golden. Remove and add the remaining cubes, and fry, carefully stirring with a dry slotted spoon, until golden, about 30 seconds. Transfer to paper towels to drain.

Chapter five

PASTA *and* RICE DISHES

PERCIATELLI *with* SHREDDED ROAST CHICKEN, SWEET ONIONS, *and* PANCETTA

Roast chicken is in good company tossed into pasta with pancetta, breadcrumbs, and onions made extra-sweet from a quick oven roast. Perciatelli is a long pasta, like spaghetti, but fatter and with a hollow center. Bucatini, spaghetti, or any other long pasta can also be used.

Good basic kitchen salt, like kosher (for water)

1½ pounds yellow onions

8 tablespoons extra-virgin olive oil

Flaky coarse sea salt

Freshly ground black pepper

½ pound flat pancetta or bacon, cut crosswise into ¾-inch pieces (see Box on page 127)

1 garlic clove, gently smashed and peeled

½ teaspoon red pepper flakes

1½ cups medium shreds roast chicken

1 pound perciatelli or other long pasta

1 cup freshly grated Parmigiano-Reggiano cheese (4½ ounces), plus more for serving

¾ cup coarse breadcrumbs, preferably homemade (see Box)

½ cup coarsely chopped fresh parsley leaves

Preheat the oven to 450°F with the rack in the middle. Bring a large pot of well-salted water to a boil.

Peel the onions, keeping the root ends intact, then cut into ⅓-inch wedges. On a rimmed baking sheet, toss the onions with 2 tablespoons of the oil, and a generous pinch of salt and pepper. Roast the onions, turning and stirring halfway through, until golden, about 20 minutes.

Meanwhile, in a large skillet, heat 2 tablespoons of the oil and the pancetta over medium heat, stirring, until the edges a begin to crisp, about 8 minutes. Transfer to a large serving bowl (big enough to toss the pasta).

Return the skillet to medium heat. Add the remaining 4 tablespoons oil, garlic, and pepper flakes. Cook over medium-low heat until the oil is fragrant, about 3 minutes. Remove the pan from the heat.

Add the onions and chicken to the skillet and stir to combine. Transfer the mixture to the bowl with the pancetta.

Cook the pasta in the boiling water until al dente, then drain and immediately add to the serving bowl. Toss with the chicken mixture, then add the cheese, breadcrumbs, and parsley in three additions, tossing between each. Season with salt and pepper. Pass extra cheese at the table.

---

making breadcrumbs

Homemade breadcrumbs taste worlds better than store-bought, and they're easy to make. Instead of throwing away stale bread, cut it into 2-inch pieces, spread out on a baking sheet, and bake in a 325°F oven until it's lightly toasted and dried, about 20 minutes. Let the bread cool, then pulse it in a food processor to make coarse or fine crumbs. Store homemade breadcrumbs in an airtight container in the refrigerator for up to three days or in the freezer for up to four months.

ROAST CHICKEN CACCIATORE
with POLENTA

Cacciatore means "hunter's style," which is likely more a reference to versions of this dish prepared with rabbit, rather than those made with chicken (both are classic). Either way, it's a fresh-tasting, meaty, and tomatoey-sweet dish that's delicious over soft, warm polenta.

Serves 4

5 tablespoons extra-virgin olive oil

1 red bell pepper, thinly sliced

1 medium yellow onion, thinly sliced

4 garlic cloves, thinly sliced

1 (28-ounce) can whole peeled tomatoes in juice (preferably San Marzano)

Fine sea salt

¼ teaspoon red pepper flakes

2½ cups large shreds roast chicken

1½ cups polenta (coarse cornmeal)

In a 5½-quart Dutch oven or heavy pot with lid, heat the oil over medium-high heat. Add the bell pepper, onion, and garlic; reduce the heat to medium-low and cook, stirring occasionally, until softened, about 10 minutes.

Add the tomatoes and their juices, ½ teaspoon salt, and the red pepper flakes; stir to combine well. Bring the mixture to a simmer, then simmer, covered, for 30 minutes.

Stir in the chicken and continue to cook, covered, for 20 minutes more.

Meanwhile, in a medium saucepan, bring 3 cups of water and ½ teaspoon salt to a boil. Whisking, add the polenta in a slow stream, then cook, stirring frequently with a long-handled wooden spoon, until the polenta is tender and very thick, about 30 minutes.

When the sauce has cooked with the chicken for 20 minutes, uncover and cook 5 minutes more. Then remove from the heat and cover to keep warm.

Serve the cacciatore with the polenta.

STROZZAPRETI *with* SPINACH-BASIL PESTO *and* RICOTTA SALATA

Serves 4

Strozzapreti, "priest strangler" in Italian, are fun twisty short pasta. Other short types, like farfalle, fusilli, orecchietti, and rotelle ("wagon wheels"), work well here, too. The combination of spinach and basil makes for a healthy, bright green pesto, and ricotta salata—a fresh-tasting, mildly salty cheese—adds a slightly nutty touch.

Good basic kitchen salt, like kosher (for water)

1 (10-ounce) bunch spinach, tough stems removed (about 5 cups packed)

1 cup packed fresh basil leaves

3 tablespoons pine nuts

1 garlic clove

Fine sea salt

6 tablespoons extra-virgin olive oil

1 pound strozzapreti or other short pasta

2½ cups finely shredded roast chicken, at room temperature

Good-quality extra-virgin olive oil for drizzling

¼ cup ricotta salata cheese, thinly shaved (2 ounces)

Bring a large pot of well-salted water to a boil.

In a food processor, combine the spinach, basil, pine nuts, garlic, and ½ teaspoon fine sea salt. With the machine running, add the oil in a slow and steady stream; purée until smooth.

Cook the pasta in the boiling water until al dente. Reserving ¼ cup of the cooking liquid, drain the pasta, then return the pasta to the pot off the heat. Immediately add the pesto and chicken, and stir to combine thoroughly. Moisten with 2 tablespoons of the pasta cooking liquid, or more, if desired.

Serve immediately, drizzled with a touch of good oil and topped with the cheese and extra salt to taste.

> *cleaning your greens*
>
> Wash spinach, basil, and other greens well before using, since even a touch of sandy grit can take away from, if not ruin, the pleasure of a good dish. A great way to wash is to plug up the sink and fill it with cold water, then plunge in the greens and swish them around. Let the greens sit, undisturbed for a few minutes, then carefully lift them out of the water, without disturbing the grit, which will have fallen to the bottom of the sink. Drain and rinse out the sink, then repeat as necessary.

FARRO PASTA *with* ROAST CHICKEN, BUTTERNUT SQUASH, *and* FRESH OREGANO

Serves 4

Roasted butternut squash pairs best with a hearty pasta, like one made from nutty-tasting farro, which balances its sweet flavor. Pasta made from white or semolina flour doesn't stand up to the task, but you can use whole-wheat pasta, if the farro type is unavailable. A short curly shape, like torchietti, catches the squash cubes nicely, though any shape will do. Try fresh marjoram in place of oregano, if you like.

1 garlic clove, gently smashed and peeled

8 tablespoons extra-virgin olive oil

1 (1¼-pound) butternut squash, peeled, seeded, and cut into ½-inch cubes (about 4 cups)

Flaky coarse sea salt

Freshly ground coarse black pepper

Good basic kitchen salt, like kosher (for water)

3 tablespoons fresh oregano leaves

½ teaspoon red pepper flakes

1 pound farro torchietti or other short farro or whole-wheat pasta (see Sources and Credits, page 170)

1½ cups medium shreds roast chicken, at room temperature

¼ cup coarsely chopped fresh parsley leaves

1½ cups freshly grated Parmigiano-Reggiano cheese (about 5 ounces)

Preheat the oven to 450°F with the rack in the middle. Line a rimmed baking sheet with parchment paper.

In a small saucepan, combine the garlic and 7 tablespoons of the oil. Heat over medium heat just until the oil begins to sizzle, then remove the pan from the heat and set aside.

On the prepared baking sheet, toss together the squash cubes, the remaining 1 tablespoon oil, and a generous pinch of coarse salt and black pepper to coat. Roast the squash, stirring once and turning the pan halfway through, until tender and golden, about 20 minutes.

Meanwhile, bring a large pot of well-salted water to a boil.

Remove the squash from the oven and, while hot, sprinkle with the oregano and pepper flakes, then put the pan on a wire rack.

Cook the pasta in the boiling water until al dente. Meanwhile, discard the garlic clove from the reserved oil and gently warm over low heat.

Reserving 2 tablespoons of the cooking liquid, drain the pasta and transfer to a large serving bowl. Add the reserved cooking liquid, warmed oil, squash, chicken, and parsley; toss to combine. Add 1 cup of the cheese and toss once more. Serve immediately, sprinkled with the remaining ½ cup cheese and salt and pepper to taste.

PASTA CARBONARA *with* ROAST CHICKEN *and* SUGAR SNAP PEAS

Chicken and peas in a carbonara is not classic, but a nice twist on this creamy, indulgent dish. The peas are a natural fit for bacon and eggs, and add a nice touch of green.

Serves 4

Good basic kitchen salt, like kosher (for water)

1 cup sugar snap peas, strings removed and snap peas cut crosswise into ¼-inch pieces

3 tablespoons extra-virgin olive oil

3 large cloves, gently smashed and peeled

½ pound thick-cut smoked bacon or flat pancetta, preferably cut in one ½-inch-thick slice, then crosswise into ¼-inch pieces (or 1-inch pieces if it is thinner)

½ cup dry white wine

1 pound spaghetti

1½ cups medium shreds roast chicken

3 large eggs, lightly beaten

1½ cups freshly grated Parmigiano-Reggiano cheese (about 5 ounces)

¼ cup finely chopped fresh parsley leaves

2 teaspoons freshly ground coarse black pepper

Bring a large pot of well-salted water to a boil.

In a medium skillet, combine the peas, oil, and garlic. Heat over medium heat until the oil is warmed and fragrant and the peas are tender yet still have a little snap, about 5 minutes. Remove the skillet from the heat. Using a slotted spoon, discard the garlic, and transfer the peas to a large serving bowl (big enough to toss the cooked pasta). Return the skillet to medium-high heat. Add the bacon and cook, stirring occasionally, until the edges are crisp, about 4 minutes, then add the wine and cook for 2 minutes more. Remove the skillet from the heat.

Cook the pasta in the boiling water until al dente. Meanwhile, add the chicken to the skillet with the bacon and oil, and gently warm over low heat.

Add the beaten eggs, ¾ cup of the cheese, the parsley, and pepper to the bowl with the peas; whisk to combine.

Drain the pasta and immediately add it to the bowl with the egg mixture, then add the chicken mixture. Quickly and thoroughly toss the pasta to coat the strands well with the sauce. Add the remaining cheese and toss once more. Serve immediately.

---

buying bacon

If you can purchase the bacon or flat pancetta for this dish from a butcher shop or good supermarket meat counter, ask for a ½-inch-thick piece, then cut the piece crosswise into ⅓-inch batons (the batons, once cooked, have salty-crisp edges and a good toothsome bite). Otherwise use a thick-cut packaged bacon (a little thinner than the first option, but still good) and cut the strips crosswise into 1-inch pieces.

BAKED MACARONI *and* CHEESE *with* ROAST CHICKEN, SMOKED MOZZARELLA, *and* ROSEMARY

There are a few steps here and maybe an extra pot or two to clean, but this mac and cheese is crazy delicious (in other words, totally worth it). Have your onion sliced, cheeses grated, chicken shredded, and herbs chopped before going to the stove, and you'll sail right through.

Serves 4 to 6

3 tablespoons unsalted butter, plus more for baking dish

Good basic kitchen salt, like kosher (for water)

½ pound penne pasta

1 tablespoon extra-virgin olive oil

1 small yellow onion, thinly sliced

Fine sea salt

1½ cups smoked mozzarella or scamorza cheese, coarsely grated (½ pound)

1½ cups medium shreds roast chicken

1 cup freshly grated Parmigiano-Reggiano cheese (about 2 ounces)

1 tablespoon finely chopped fresh rosemary leaves

3 tablespoons unbleached all-purpose flour

2½ cups whole milk, heated to a simmer

2 garlic cloves, peeled

Freshly ground black pepper

Preheat the oven to 450°F with the rack in the middle. Grease a 1½-quart gratin or baking dish with butter.

Bring a large pot of well-salted water to a boil. Cook the pasta until al dente, then drain and run under cold water. Transfer to a large bowl.

Heat the oil in a medium skillet over medium heat. Add the onion and a pinch of fine sea salt, reduce the heat to medium-low and cook, stirring occasionally, until softened and lightly golden, about 10 minutes.

Add the onion to the pasta and stir to combine, then add the mozzarella, chicken, ⅔ cup of the Parmigiano-Reggiano, and rosemary. Stir again to combine.

Melt the butter in a heavy saucepan over medium-low heat. Add the flour and cook over low heat, whisking, for 3 minutes. Add the hot milk in a fast stream, whisking vigorously, then whisk in the garlic cloves and 1½ teaspoons salt. Bring the mixture to a simmer, whisking, then reduce the heat and very gently simmer, whisking occasionally, until the béchamel is thickened (the sauce should thickly coat the back of a spoon), about 10 minutes. Discard the garlic before adding the béchamel to the pasta, along with generous pepper, and stir to combine thoroughly.

Transfer the mixture to the gratin and smooth the top. Sprinkle with the remaining Parmigiano-Reggiano and more pepper. Bake until bubbling and golden, 12 to 15 minutes. Let sit for 15 minutes before serving.

get the good stuff and grate your own

Always use good-quality Parmigiano-Reggiano cheese, purchase the cheese in a whole block (versus grated), and grate it just before using. Pre-grated options might be convenient, but they greatly compromise flavor and are more expensive to boot.

WHOLE-WHEAT SPAGHETTI *with* ROAST CHICKEN, SHREDDED BRUSSELS SPROUTS, *and* PARMESAN

Most people who say they don't like Brussels sprouts actually love Brussels sprouts, they just don't know it yet. The key is proper cooking, which brings out the sweet buttery goodness of the vegetable (this recipe offers just one of several techniques). Here, the thinner the sprouts are sliced, the more sweet and tender they will be.

Serves 4 to 6

Good basic kitchen salt, like kosher (for water)

1¼ pounds Brussels sprouts, discolored leaves discarded and stems intact

2 tablespoons unsalted butter

6 tablespoons extra-virgin olive oil, plus more for drizzling

2 garlic cloves, thinly sliced

1 pound whole-wheat spaghetti

1 cup chicken broth, preferably homemade (page 100), heated to a simmer

1½ cups sliced roast chicken

2 cups freshly grated Parmigiano-Reggiano cheese (about 7 ounces)

Freshly ground black pepper

Flaky coarse sea salt

---

smart slicing

To slice any round veggie safely, use an adjustable-blade slicer, with the safety guard, or, using a sharp knife, cut a slice or two to create a flat edge. Put the flat side down on the cutting board to secure a stable position so the vegetable does not roll while you cut.

Bring a large pot of well-salted water to a boil.

Holding each Brussels sprout by the stem end, cut into very thin slices using an adjustable-blade slicer or thinly slice with a good sharp knife.

Heat the butter and 2 tablespoons oil in a 5½- to 7-quart Dutch oven or heavy pot with lid over medium heat until the butter is melted. Add the Brussels sprouts and a generous pinch of coarse salt. Reduce the heat to low, cover the pot, and cook, stirring frequently, for 5 minutes. Add ¼ cup water and continue to cook, covered, stirring occasionally, until Brussels sprouts are tender but still firm to the bite, 15 to 20 minutes more.

Meanwhile, heat the garlic and the remaining 4 tablespoons oil in a small skillet or saucepan over low heat, swirling the pan occasionally, until fragrant and lightly golden, 5 to 6 minutes. Remove from the heat. When the Brussels sprouts are done, let them sit, covered, off the heat.

Cook the pasta in the boiling water until al dente. Reserving ½ cup of the cooking liquid, drain the pasta and transfer to a large serving bowl. Immediately add the Brussels sprouts, broth, garlic and oil, and toss together. Add the chicken and 1½ cups of the cheese. Toss together. Add the cooking liquid to moisten, if desired. Serve the pasta immediately, drizzled with extra oil and sprinkled with generous black pepper, the remaining ½ cup cheese, and a little coarse salt on top.

FARROTO *with* ROAST CHICKEN *and* HERBS

Serves 4

I love farroto, a dish cooked like risotto, but with farro in place of rice. Hot broth is added to the grain little by little until it is tender, creamy, and deeply flavorful. A conscious eye and stirring as needed are all that's required. For proper cooking, keep the broth covered, continuously simmering, if necessary, so it stays hot. You want a tender, yet firm (not overcooked, mushy) farroto. Letting the finished dish sit covered for 5 minutes before serving completes the cooking. Trust the process and the dish will be perfect.

2 tablespoons extra-virgin olive oil, plus more for drizzling

2 tablespoons unsalted butter

1 cup yellow onion, finely chopped (from 1 small to medium)

1 garlic clove, finely chopped

Flaky coarse sea salt

2 cups farro (see Sources and Credits, page 170)

½ cup dry white wine

4½ cups chicken broth, preferably homemade (page 100), heated to a simmer

½ teaspoon fine sea salt

¾ cup freshly grated Parmigiano-Reggiano cheese (about 3 ounces), plus more for serving

1½ cups medium shreds roast chicken

⅓ cup chopped mixed fresh herb leaves, such as basil, marjoram, parsley, thyme, and chives

Freshly ground black pepper

Heat the oil and butter in a heavy large saucepan or Dutch oven over medium heat until the butter is melted. Add the onion, garlic, and a generous pinch of coarse salt. Reduce the heat to low and cook, stirring occasionally, until softened (do not brown), about 7 minutes. Add the farro, stir to coat with the oil mixture, and cook, stirring occasionally, for 2 minutes more.

Add the wine and cook, stirring frequently, until the wine evaporates, about 5 minutes. Then add ½ cup of the hot broth and cook, stirring occasionally, until the broth is almost fully evaporated (when the spoon scrapes the bottom of the pan, you should see hardly any liquid, though you do not want the farro to stick to the bottom). Cook this "low and slow." Each addition of broth should take about 7 minutes to fully evaporate; reduce the heat if necessary. Continue to add the broth, ½ cups at a time, until the farroto is tender, yet still firm to the bite (you should have about 1 cup broth left over), then remove from the heat, stir in the fine sea salt, cover, and let sit for 5 minutes.

Stir in the cheese, ¼ cup at a time, then stir in the chicken and herbs. Add ⅓ to ½ cup of the remaining broth to moisten the farroto, then spoon into shallow bowls. Spoon a couple teaspoons broth over and around the edges of each serving, drizzle with oil, and sprinkle with more cheese, coarse salt, and pepper.

CHORIZO, SHRIMP, and ROAST CHICKEN PAELLA with GREEN OLIVE-PIMENTO AIOLI

Serves 4

Spain's Bomba and Calasparra rices are the best varieties for paella because they absorb more liquid than other short-grain types, and so take on more flavor. Risotto rice works well, too.

2 tablespoons extra-virgin olive oil

2 cups finely chopped yellow onions

4 ounces fully cooked Mexican or Spanish chorizo, thinly sliced crosswise

4 garlic cloves, thinly sliced

2 cups short-grain rice, preferably Bomba or Calasparra (see Sources and Credits, page 170)

1 teaspoon saffron threads

½ cup dry white wine

2 cups bottled clam juice

1½ cups chicken broth, preferably homemade (see page 100)

½ teaspoon paprika, preferably Pimentón de la Vera (see Sources and Credits, page 170)

1½ cups frozen peas, not thawed

1 (7-ounce) jar roasted sliced pimento peppers with juice

½ pound large shrimp, peeled and deveined

1¾ cups medium shreds roast chicken

AIOLI

1 cup mayonnaise

1 large lemon

1 large garlic clove, finely chopped

3 tablespoons finely chopped pimento-stuffed green olives

Fine sea salt

Preheat the oven to 450°F with the rack in the lower third of the oven.

In a 13-inch paella pan or a wide heavy pot, heat the oil over medium-high heat. Stir in the onions, chorizo, and garlic, reduce the heat to medium, and cook, stirring occasionally, until the onion and garlic are softened, about 10 minutes.

Stir in the rice and saffron and cook until the rice is opaque, about 3 minutes. Add the wine and cook until evaporated, about 1 minute more. Add the clam juice, broth, and paprika; bring the liquid to a simmer. Remove from the heat and stir in the peas and the pimento peppers and their juices.

If you are not using a paella pan, transfer the rice mixture to a 15x10x2-inch baking dish and cover tightly with foil. Otherwise, cover the paella pan with the lid. Bake the paella for 35 minutes, then stir in the shrimp and chicken, and continue to cook, covered, for 10 minutes more.

Meanwhile, make the aioli: Put the mayonnaise into a bowl. Finely zest the lemon into the bowl, holding the zester close so that you capture the flavorful oil that sprays from the lemon as you zest. Squeeze 2 tablespoons of the juice from the lemon and add it to the mayonnaise mixture. Add the garlic and olives and stir together to combine. Season with salt. Serve the paella with the aioli.

CHICKEN JAMBALAYA *with* ANDOUILLE SAUSAGE *and* BACON

Serves 6

I lucked out in countless ways when I met my husband, Steve, not the least of which being that he's a born-and-bred Louisianan, so he knows his po' boys from his pig roasts. It took a few years of marriage before I wandered into Steve's jambalaya territory, and I still call him to the stove when I'm making this spicy dish. Though most jambalayas call for white rice, I prefer the nuttiness of brown.

1 pound andouille sausage, cut crosswise into ⅓-inch pieces

6 ounces bacon, cut crosswise into 1-inch pieces

1 tablespoon extra-virgin olive oil

2 medium yellow onions, cut into ¼-inch dice

2 large green bell peppers, cut into ¼-inch dice

4 celery stalks, cut crosswise into ¼-inch pieces

4 garlic cloves, thinly sliced

2 cups brown basmati rice

2 teaspoons fine sea salt

2 teaspoons paprika, preferably Pimentón de la Vera (see Sources and Credits, page 170)

1 teaspoon dried thyme

1 teaspoon freshly ground black pepper

½ teaspoon cayenne pepper

1 (28-ounce) can whole peeled tomatoes in juice (preferably San Marzano)

3¼ cups chicken broth, preferably homemade (page 100)

3 cups medium shreds roast chicken

1 bunch scallions, trimmed and thinly sliced

In a 5½-quart heavy pot or Dutch oven, combine the sausage, bacon, and oil; cook over medium-high heat, stirring occasionally, until the bacon is crisp and the sausage is golden, about 8 minutes. Add the onions, reduce the heat to medium, and cook, stirring occasionally, until softened, about 5 minutes.

Add the bell peppers, celery, and garlic; cook, stirring occasionally, until the vegetables are softened, about 10 minutes.

Add the rice, salt, paprika, thyme, black pepper, and cayenne; stir well to combine. Cook, stirring frequently until the rice is toasted, about 3 minutes, then stir in the tomatoes and their juices, the broth, and the chicken. Bring to a boil, then reduce the heat to medium-low and cook, covered, until the rice is tender and most of the liquid is absorbed, about 1 hour.

Remove the pot from the heat and let stand, covered, for 10 minutes, then stir in the scallions.

TOMATO-CHICKPEA MASALA *with* CHICKEN, YOGURT, *and* CILANTRO

Steve and I love Indian flavors. When we're pressed for time during the week, this is a favorite quick dinner to make, and simple, because it's mostly made up of pantry ingredients. Try it without the chicken, when you want a vegetarian dish.

Serves 6

1½ cups long-grain white rice

Fine sea salt

3 tablespoons extra-virgin olive oil

2 tablespoons unsalted butter

2 medium yellow onions, finely chopped

4 garlic cloves, thinly sliced

2 tablespoons fresh ginger, finely chopped

1½ tablespoons garam masala

⅛ teaspoon cayenne pepper

2 (28-ounce) cans whole peeled tomatoes in juice (preferably San Marzano)

2 (15-ounce) cans chickpeas, rinsed and drained

¾ cup coconut milk

1½ teaspoons sugar

1¾ cups sliced roast chicken, at room temperature

½ cup plain yogurt

¼ cup coarsely chopped fresh cilantro leaves

1 lemon, cut into wedges

Bring 3 cups of water just to a boil in a large heavy saucepan. Add the rice and ¾ teaspoon salt; return to a boil, then cover, reduce the heat to low, and cook, undisturbed, until the water is absorbed and rice is tender, about 15 minutes.

Meanwhile, heat the oil and butter in a 5-quart Dutch oven or heavy pot over medium-low heat until the butter is melted. Add the onions, garlic, ginger, garam masala, and cayenne and cook, stirring occasionally, until the onion is softened, about 5 minutes. Add the tomatoes and their juices, and the chickpeas. Using a potato masher or the back of a large wooden spoon, mash about half of the chickpeas.

Bring the mixture to a simmer and cook, stirring occasionally, for 10 minutes, then stir in the coconut milk, sugar, and 1¼ teaspoons salt, and cook for 5 minutes more. Adjust seasoning, if desired. Serve the masala over the rice, with chicken, spoonfuls of yogurt, cilantro, and a squeeze of lemon juice on top.

KOREAN RICE BOWL *with* ROAST CHICKEN, SPINACH, CARROTS, ZUCCHINI, RED CHILE PASTE, *and a* FRIED EGG

Serves 4

This is one of my favorite dishes; it's very clean tasting and beautiful and an easy, fun way to make Korean food at home. The vegetables and a fried egg are separately arranged over steaming hot rice. To eat it, you break up the egg then take bites of each element, alone or mixed together.

1 tablespoon sesame seeds

Good basic kitchen salt, like kosher (for water)

1 pound fresh spinach, stemmed

2 cups sushi rice, also called pearl rice or Japanese rice (see Sources and Credits, page 170)

4 tablespoons plus ½ teaspoon sesame oil

2 garlic cloves, finely chopped

Fine sea salt

2 medium carrots, julienned

1 large zucchini, julienned

5 ounces shiitake mushrooms (about 6 large), stems trimmed and caps cut into ¼-inch slices

1⅓ cups small shreds roast chicken, at room temperature

½ teaspoon soy sauce, plus more to taste

4 large eggs

2 tablespoons extra-virgin olive oil

2 cups coarsely chopped kimchi (see Sources and Credits, page 170)

In a small skillet, heat the sesame seeds over medium-low heat, shaking the skillet back and forth, until the seeds are fragrant and lightly golden, about 3 minutes. Transfer the seeds to a plate.

Bring a large pot of salted water to a boil. Add the spinach and cook for 1 minute, then drain. When the spinach is cool enough to handle, using your hands, squeeze all of the excess liquid out, then set aside.

Rinse the rice in cold water, then drain. In a large, heavy saucepan, cover the rice with 2¼ cups water and add a generous pinch of fine salt. Bring to a boil, then cover and cook over very low heat until the rice is tender and the water is absorbed, 18 to 20 minutes. (The rice can also be cooked in a rice cooker, using the same proportions of rice and water. Keep the rice hot until you are ready to serve.)

While the rice is cooking, heat 1 tablespoon of the sesame oil in a medium skillet over medium heat. Add a quarter of the garlic, reduce the heat to very low and cook, stirring once or twice, until fragrant and softened, about 30 seconds. Add the spinach and a pinch of fine salt. Using a wooden spoon to stir and break up the clumps, cook for 1 minute, then transfer to a large plate.

Wipe the skillet dry with a paper towel, then add 1 tablespoon sesame oil and heat over medium heat. Add a second quarter of the garlic, reduce the heat to very low and cook, stirring, for 30 seconds. Add the carrots and a pinch of fine sea salt, and cook, stirring occasionally, until the carrots are tender but still a little firm to the bite, about 5 minutes. Transfer to the plate with the spinach, keeping the vegetables separate.

Torn sheets of nori (see Sources and Credits, page 170)

2 large scallions, trimmed and thinly sliced on a long diagonal

***Kochujang* (Korean chile-soy-bean paste), see Sources and Credits, page 170**

---

sushi rice

Sushi rice is a fragrant, sticky short-grain variety. Though sometimes referred to as sweet rice or glutinous rice, it is neither sweet nor glutinous. You may find that using a good rice cooker makes sushi rice easier to cook, but, with just a little practice, you'll see that the stove-top version is not very hard. A bit of the rice may stick to the pot but that's okay.

Repeat the process above, cooking the zucchini and the mushrooms separately and in the same manner, using 1 tablespoon sesame oil, a quarter of the garlic, and a pinch fine salt for each. The mushrooms and the zucchini will require 3 to 4 minutes.

In a bowl, toss together the chicken, soy sauce, and the remaining ½ teaspoon sesame oil.

When the rice is ready, remove the pot from the heat and let stand, covered, for 5 to 10 minutes.

Break the eggs into a bowl (if you are uncomfortable with your egg-cracking skills, crack each egg into a small bowl, to ensure that the yolks remain unbroken). Heat the olive oil in a 12-inch nonstick skillet over medium-high heat until it shimmers. Pour in the eggs and cook, undisturbed, until the whites begin to set, then, using a spatula to lift up an edge of the cooked whites to let as much raw egg white as possible flow underneath, cook about 2 minutes more (the top and yolks will still be very loose).

Spoon the rice into four large shallow bowls. Place 1 fried egg in each bowl, on top of the rice. Arrange the spinach, carrots, zucchini, mushrooms, chicken, kimchi, and nori around the edge of each bowl. Spoon about 1 teaspoon *kochujang* into each bowl, then sprinkle with the scallions and sesame seeds. Pass more *kochujang* at the table.

Chapter six

BRUNCH, LUNCH, and DINNER

ROASTED CHERRY TOMATO, CHICKEN, CHÈVRE, *and* CIABATTA BREAKFAST SANDWICH

Serves 4

I call this a breakfast sandwich, but, since eggs are great for lunch and dinner, too, it's really an anytime-of-day affair. Rosemary ciabatta (a soft Italian white bread) is especially tasty here. Plain ciabatta, a nice sourdough, or a rustic country loaf works, too.

¾ pound cherry tomatoes (about 25)

1 tablespoon extra-virgin olive oil

Flaky coarse sea salt

Freshly ground black pepper

½ loaf ciabatta bread, cut into 2 (approximately 4x4-inch) pieces and split

1 tablespoon white vinegar

4 large eggs

Good-quality extra-virgin olive oil for drizzling

10 ounces sliced roast chicken (about 8 slices), at room temperature

3 ounces Tomme Fleur Verte or other soft goat cheese (see Box)

3 to 4 tablespoons finely chopped chives

Preheat the oven to 450°F with the rack in the middle. Line a baking sheet with parchment paper.

Arrange the tomatoes in a single layer on the prepared baking sheet. Drizzle with the oil and sprinkle generously with salt and pepper. Roast until the tomatoes collapse and are just beginning to blister, 12 to 14 minutes. Meanwhile, lightly toast or grill the bread.

Add enough water to fill up a wide heavy skillet or saucepan (about 9 inches wide) to a depth of 1½ inches, add vinegar, and bring to a simmer. Break 1 egg into a small bowl or cup and slide the egg into the water. Repeat with each remaining egg, spacing them evenly in the skillet, and poach at a bare simmer until the whites are firm and the yolks are cooked as you like them (2 to 4 minutes). Transfer the cooked eggs to paper towels using a slotted spoon.

Remove the tomatoes from the oven. Make sandwiches by putting the pieces of bread onto 4 individual plates and drizzling each with the good-quality oil, then stacking with chicken, eggs, tomatoes (reserving any juices from the pan), and cheese. Drizzle once more with the good-quality oil, then spoon any juices from the tomatoes over the top, and sprinkle with the chives, salt, and pepper. Serve warm.

> *choice of chèvre*
>
> Tomme Fleur Verte, an herb- and pink peppercorn-seasoned soft, tangy young cheese from Périgord in France is a nice cheese in this sandwich, but you can use any soft goat cheese you like.

SWEET POTATO *and* ROAST CHICKEN HASH *with* SUNNY-SIDE UP EGGS

~~~~~~

This elemental dish, made with just a few ingredients, but, oh so good, is one of my favorite and easy weekend breakfasts.

Serves 4

1½ pounds sweet potatoes, cut in half crosswise, then cut lengthwise into ½-inch wedges

5 tablespoons extra-virgin olive oil

½ teaspoon flaky coarse sea salt, plus more for the eggs

4 scallions, trimmed and thinly sliced

1 whole dried red chile, crumbled, or ¼ teaspoon red pepper flakes

2½ cups large shreds roast chicken, at room temperature

4 large eggs

Freshly ground black pepper

Preheat the oven to 450°F with the rack in the middle.

Heat a rimmed baking sheet in the oven for 10 minutes. Meanwhile, in a large bowl, stir together the potatoes, 3 tablespoons oil, and the ½ teaspoon salt.

Using oven mitts (it's easy to forget that the pan is hot), remove the pan from oven and immediately spread the potatoes and their oil (use a rubber spatula to get all of the oil from the bowl onto the pan) in a single layer onto the pan.

Roast the potatoes for 15 minutes then, using a metal spatula, loosen, stir, and turn the potatoes. Continue roasting for 5 minutes more, then sprinkle the scallions and crumbled chile over the potatoes, stir once or twice to distribute evenly, and continue roasting until the potatoes are golden and tender, about 5 minutes more.

Remove the pan from the oven, add the chicken and, using the spatula, turn and stir the mixture to combine.

Break the eggs into a bowl (if you are uncomfortable with your egg-cracking skills, crack each egg into a small bowl, to ensure that the yolks remain unbroken). Heat the remaining 2 tablespoons oil in a 12-inch nonstick skillet over medium-high heat until it shimmers. Pour in the eggs and cook, undisturbed, until the whites begin to set, then, using a spatula to lift up an edge of the cooked whites to let as much raw egg white as possible flow underneath, cook about 2 minutes more. Season with salt and pepper. Serve the eggs over the hash.

ROAST CHICKEN, SWEET CORN, *and* POBLANO PEPPER QUESADILLAS

Quesadillas make a fun and easy weeknight meal. We serve these with little glasses of El Tesoro blanco tequila over crushed ice with a generous squeeze of fresh lime juice, though a glass of white wine is also nice. When fresh corn is not in season, use frozen corn, or leave it out.

Serves 4

1 large poblano chile

2 tablespoons plus 1½ teaspoons extra-virgin olive oil

2 ears corn, kernels cut from cob (about 1½ cups)

1 medium yellow onion, finely chopped

2 garlic cloves, thinly sliced

¾ teaspoon fine sea salt

¼ teaspoon ground cumin

8 (8-inch) flour tortillas

⅓ pound sharp cheddar cheese, coarsely grated (about 1 cup packed)

⅓ pound Monterey Jack cheese, coarsely grated (about 1 cup packed)

1¾ cups medium roast chicken shreds

¾ pound grape tomatoes, halved

⅓ cup coarsely chopped fresh cilantro leaves

Hot sauce

Preheat the oven to 300°F with the rack in the middle.

Char the chile directly over a gas burner set on high, on a grill pan over high heat, or on a hot grill, turning frequently, until blackened and blistered on all sides. Transfer to a large bowl and cover tightly with plastic wrap; let sit for 10 minutes. Peel, seed, and coarsely chop the chile.

Heat 2 tablespoons of the oil in large nonstick skillet over medium-high heat. Add the chile, corn, onion, garlic, salt, and cumin; stir to combine. Reduce the heat to medium and cook until softened, about 8 minutes. Transfer to a bowl. Wipe the skillet dry with a paper towel.

Place 4 tortillas on your work surface. Leaving a ½ inch border, sprinkle a quarter of the corn mixture, a quarter of each cheese, then a quarter of the chicken, tomatoes, and cilantro on each tortilla. Top each with a second tortilla and press to adhere.

In a large nonstick skillet, heat 1 teaspoon oil over medium-high heat. Add 1 quesadilla; cook until the filling is warmed through and the cheese is melted, about 2 minutes per side. (If corn kernels fall out from inside the tortillas as the quesadillas cook, remove the kernels from the pan. Otherwise the hot kernels will pop out of the pan.) Transfer to a baking sheet and put in the oven. Repeat with the remaining quesadillas and ½ teaspoon oil.

Cut the quesadillas into quarters. Serve with hot sauce.

> *for those who like crema*
>
> If you like, you can make a Mexican-style *crema*, or loose sour cream, to serve with this dish. Stir together sour cream with fresh lime zest and juice, and salt to taste.

CUBAN RICE *with* CHICKEN

Some say this dish is from Cuba, others claim Spain. Either way, it's one of the best brunches I know. The combination of sweet (from the skillet-cooked banana) and savory (chicken, rice, tomato sauce, and egg) may seem unusual, but, in fact, it works brilliantly. Serve this with a pot of *café con leche*.

Serves 4

1 cup long-grain white rice

Fine sea salt

1 (28-ounce) can whole peeled tomatoes (preferably San Marzano)

1 garlic clove, peeled

Sugar (optional)

2 tablespoons plus 2 teaspoons extra-virgin olive oil

2 large scallions, or 4 skinny ones, trimmed and thinly sliced

½ teaspoon dried oregano

Heaping ⅛ teaspoon ground cumin

1½ cups small shreds roast chicken

2 large firm-ripe bananas

4 large eggs

Bring 2 cups of water to a boil in a medium saucepan. Add the rice and ½ teaspoon salt, reduce to a gentle simmer, cover, and cook until the water is absorbed and the rice is tender, about 15 minutes. Let the rice sit, uncovered for 5 minutes, then fluff with a fork.

Drain the tomatoes, reserving the juices for another use. Combine the tomatoes and garlic in a blender and purée until the salsa is smooth. Add a pinch of sugar to sweeten, if desired.

In a large nonstick skillet, heat 1 tablespoon oil over medium-high heat. Add the scallions, oregano, and cumin. Reduce the heat to medium and cook, stirring occasionally, for 1 minute, then add the chicken and a pinch of salt, stir well, and cook for 1 minute more. Add to the rice and stir to combine. Adjust the seasoning, then cover to keep warm.

Peel the bananas and cut them in half crosswise, then cut again in half lengthwise.

Wipe the skillet dry with a paper towel, then add 2 teaspoons oil and heat over medium-high heat until hot but not smoking. Add the banana pieces, flat-side down, and cook until browned, 2 to 3 minutes, then turn and cook for 30 seconds more. Transfer to a plate.

Wipe the skillet dry and fry the eggs in the remaining 1 tablespoon oil. Season with salt and pepper.

Spoon the rice onto 4 individual plates and top each with an egg. Serve with the bananas and salsa.

ROAST CHICKEN MELT *with* PARSLEY PESTO, ROASTED RED ONION, *and* SHARP CHEDDAR CHEESE

Serves 4

Friends often ask me about uses for leftover fresh herbs. Turning them into pesto is one of the best: of course, to toss with pasta, but a nice spread for sandwiches, crostini, or crackers, too. Basil or cilantro can be used in place of parsley, if you like. This is a "glass of white wine" type of sandwich—great for lunch or dinner, with a salad alongside.

2 tablespoons pine nuts

3 red onions, peeled and cut crosswise into ¼-inch slices, rings kept intact

¼ cup plus 2 tablespoons extra-virgin olive oil

Flaky coarse sea salt

Freshly ground black pepper

2 cups packed fresh parsley leaves

1 tablespoon fresh lemon juice

1 garlic clove, peeled

Fine sea salt

4 (½-inch-thick) slices bread from a large rustic boule, grilled or lightly toasted

½ pound sliced roast chicken

6 ounces sharp cheddar cheese, thinly sliced

Preheat the oven to 425°F with the rack in the middle. Line a baking sheet with parchment paper.

Put the pine nuts into a small skillet and heat over low heat, occasionally shaking the pan back and forth, until the nuts are lightly golden, about 8 minutes. Transfer to a plate.

Put the onions on the prepared baking sheet, keeping the rings intact. Drizzle with 2 tablespoons oil and season with coarse salt and pepper. Roast until the edges of the onions are golden, 13 to 15 minutes.

Meanwhile, combine the pine nuts, parsley, remaining ¼ cup oil, lemon juice, 1 tablespoon water, garlic, and ¼ teaspoon fine salt in the bowl of a food processor; purée until smooth.

Transfer the onions to a wire rack to cool slightly. Increase the oven temperature to broil.

Arrange the bread slices in a single layer on another baking sheet. Spread 1 tablespoon of the pesto onto each slice. Top with the chicken and sprinkle with coarse salt and pepper. Top with half of the onion slices, then cover with the cheese, tucking any exposed onion pieces under the cheese to prevent burning. Broil the sandwiches about 4 inches from the heat just until the cheese is bubbling, about 1 minute.

Dollop the warm sandwiches with the remaining pesto, top with the remaining onion slices, and sprinkle with coarse salt. Serve warm.

ROAST CHICKEN MAYO SANDWICH 3 WAYS

Mayo. Most people either love it or hate it. If you love it, you also likely have a favorite brand. I'm a Hellmann's girl.

ROAST CHICKEN MAYO BAGUETTE

This is the "jambon beurre" of chicken sandwiches: incredibly simple, and perfect just that way.

Serves 4

4 (6-inch-long) baguette pieces, halved lengthwise

Your favorite mayonnaise

1 pound sliced roast chicken

Flaky coarse sea salt

Lightly toast or grill the baguette halves.

Spread the bread with a good slathering of mayonnaise. Layer the chicken slices onto the bottom halves of the bread, and sprinkle with salt. Cover with the top halves of bread.

ROAST CHICKEN BRIOCHE SANDWICH
with LEMON MAYO and BASIL LEAVES

Citrusy mayo and fresh basil leaves give this sandwich a spring-like feel. Use thinner slices of bread to make it like a tea sandwich.

Serves 4

¾ cup plus 1 tablespoon mayonnaise

2 tablespoons fresh lemon juice

Fine sea salt

Freshly ground black pepper

1 pound sliced roast chicken

16 large fresh basil leaves, torn (or more leaves, if small)

8 (½-inch) slices brioche bread

In a bowl, stir together the mayonnaise, lemon juice, and a generous pinch of salt and pepper.

Place four slices of bread on four individual plates. Add a layer of the chicken, and basil. Dollop with the mayonnaise, then top with four more slices of bread.

ROAST CHICKEN SANDWICH
with "GRIBICHE MAYO"

Traditional *sauce gribiche* (*oui, c'est Français*) is not a mayonnaise, though it shares similar traits. It's made with a hard-cooked egg yolk (not raw) and mashed (not whisked) with olive oil. Cooked egg white, capers, and herbs are added; it's delicious and typically served with cold fish. Here, it's done as a mayo, yet deconstructed, since it looks prettiest that way.

Serves 4

2 large eggs, in their shells

1 teaspoon whole black peppercorns

½ cup mayonnaise

7 large cornichons, or more small ones, thinly sliced on a long diagonal

4 slices good-quality sliced, packaged white bread

4 Bibb lettuce leaves, or small Boston lettuce leaves from the inner heart

1¼ cups small to medium shreds roast chicken

2 scallions, trimmed and thinly sliced on a long diagonal

1 to 2 tablespoons capers, preferably salt-packed, rinsed, soaked in cold water for 10 minutes, then rinsed again

Flaky coarse sea salt

Bring a medium saucepan of water to a boil. Gently lower the eggs into the water and boil for 10 minutes. Remove from the water and put into a bowl filled with ice water; let sit for 2 minutes, then peel. Cut off the ends of the eggs, so that your slices will lay flat, then slice the eggs crosswise into 6 slices each (you can eat the ends or tuck them into the sandwiches, as you like—cook's prerogative).

In a mortar and pestle or, using the heel of your hand on the side of a chef's knife, coarsely crack the black peppercorns.

Stir together the mayonnaise and all but 12 slices of the cornichons. Put the bread slices onto four individual plates. Place a lettuce leaf on each slice then divide the mayonnaise mixture among the leaves. Top with the chicken, egg slices, reserved cornichon slices, scallions, capers, salt, and cracked pepper.

MIDDLE EASTERN ROAST CHICKEN PITA
with HUMMUS *and* CARROT SLAW

Serves 4

Rich creamy spreads, tart pickles, heady spices, crunchy salads, and often a little meat make up most Middle Eastern pita sandwiches. The fun is choosing the fillings to stuff inside. So I hope you'll use this recipe as a road map, and vary it as you please. Try *labneh* (Middle Eastern yogurt cheese) mixed with chopped mint leaves; or baba ghanoush, in place of hummus; wilted shredded turnips, rutabaga, or kohlrabi instead of carrots. Add tender spinach or arugula leaves, dressed with olive oil and salt, or chopped cucumber, tomato, onion, and herbs. Sprinkle on pitted olives, fried or caramelized onions, or cooked lentils. Whatever you do, it's a messy affair, so be sure to have plenty of napkins on hand.

½ pound carrots, julienned or coarsely shredded

2 tablespoons fresh lemon juice

¾ teaspoon fine sea salt

1 garlic clove, finely chopped

⅛ teaspoon ground cumin

2 tablespoons extra-virgin olive oil

¾ cup hummus

4 (6-inch) whole-wheat or white pita breads, halved

1 cup medium shreds roast chicken, at room temperature

Persian pickles and/or other pickled vegetables, such as green beans, okra, baby eggplant, or turnips, larger pickles cut lengthwise into halves or quarters

½ cup coarsely chopped fresh parsley, mint, or cilantro leaves

Spicy pickled peppers, thinly sliced crosswise (optional)

Hot sauce (optional)

In a bowl, toss together the carrots, lemon juice, salt, garlic, and cumin. Let the mixture stand for 10 minutes, then add the oil and stir to combine.

Spread 1½ tablespoons of the hummus into each pita half, then divide the carrot slaw and chicken among the sandwiches. Tuck the Persian pickles into the sandwiches and sprinkle with the parsley. Top with the pickled peppers and drizzle with hot sauce, if desired.

a profusion of pickles, and pillowy pita

Heaps of delicious pickled vegetables, such as beets, turnips, baby eggplant, and more, can be purchased at good Middle Eastern food shops or delis (where you will also find high-quality, soft, pillowy pita), or try pickled green beans or okra from any good supermarket or specialty food shop.

ROAST CHICKEN BAHN MI *with* PICKLED CABBAGE, CILANTRO, *and* CUCUMBER

Serves 4

This zippy Vietnamese sandwich has so much going for it: rich meats, tangy pickled cabbage, spicy chile sauce, creamy mayo, and a vibrant mix of fresh herbs all packed into a soft baguette. Bahn mi can be made with various fillings, succulent slow-cooked fatty pork or pork pâté being among the most popular. Roast chicken is a leaner option, though with a thick slab or two of chicken pâté and a slathering of mayo, it's both flavorful and indulgent.

2 teaspoons whole coriander seeds

¼ cup plus 2 tablespoons red wine vinegar

1½ tablespoons sugar

¾ teaspoon fine sea salt

2 cups thinly sliced red cabbage

1 medium red onion, very thinly sliced

2 serrano chiles, seeded and thinly sliced crosswise

4 (6-inch-long) baguette pieces, halved lengthwise

4 to 8 tablespoons mayonnaise

Chile-garlic sauce (see Sources and Credits, page 170)

3 cups sliced roast chicken with skin

4 ounces chicken or other loaf-style pâté

½ medium cucumber, peeled, seeded, and thinly sliced lengthwise

1 cup fresh cilantro leaves

½ cup fresh mint leaves

2 scallions, trimmed and thinly sliced

2 tablespoons soy sauce

Put the coriander seeds in a small skillet. Heat over low heat, occasionally shaking the pan back and forth, until the seeds are fragrant and lightly toasted, about 3 minutes. Transfer to a cutting board, and let cool for a few minutes, then press the seeds with the side of a chef's knife to crack.

Combine the coriander, vinegar, sugar, and salt in a large bowl; whisk together to combine. Add the cabbage, onion, and chiles; toss the vegetables to coat with the vinegar mixture, and let stand, stirring occasionally, for 30 minutes.

Drain the pickled cabbage mixture. Pull enough bread from inside each bread half to leave a ½-inch-thick shell. Spread the mayonnaise on the cut sides of the bread, then dollop with chile-garlic sauce to taste. Top with the chicken, pâté, cucumber, pickled cabbage mixture, cilantro and mint leaves, and scallions. Drizzle the soy sauce over the top, then close the sandwiches.

CUBAN ROAST CHICKEN SANDWICHES
with MOJO SAUCE

A citrus sauce spiked with garlic and cumin, mojo makes a great addition to this tasty pressed Cuban sandwich, made with shreds of roast chicken in place of the classic pork.

Serves 4

1 garlic clove

¼ teaspoon fine sea salt

¼ cup fresh orange juice

2 tablespoons fresh lime juice

¼ teaspoon freshly ground black pepper

⅛ teaspoon ground cumin

1⅓ cups small shreds roast chicken, at room temperature

3 teaspoons Dijon mustard

½ long loaf soft Italian bread, cut into quarters crosswise and split lengthwise, or 4 (2-ounce) soft rolls, split lengthwise

3 ounces Swiss cheese, thinly sliced

4 ounces Virginia ham, thinly sliced

¼ pound sour pickles, cut crosswise into ¼-inch slices

2 tablespoons unsalted butter, melted

Use the side of your knife and the blade to alternately chop and gently scrape the garlic and salt together, until you have a garlic paste. Transfer to a medium bowl. Add the orange juice, lime juice, pepper, and cumin, and whisk the mojo sauce to combine. Add the chicken and mix to thoroughly combine.

Spread the mustard on the cut sides of the bottom halves of the bread, then layer with the cheese, ham, pickles, and chicken. Cover the sandwiches with the bread tops and gently press.

Heat a large cast-iron skillet over medium heat. Brush the sandwiches with the melted butter and put into the skillet; top with a smaller heavy skillet. Reduce the heat to low and cook, turning once, until the rolls are crispy on the outside, the meat is warmed through, and the cheese is starting to melt, about 8 minutes.

MOROCCAN CARROT *and* ROAST CHICKEN TART

Squares of this tart match well with martinis, and they also make a nice lunch or a light dinner, with a salad alongside. Harissa is a North African chile paste, made with garlic, cumin, coriander, and caraway. Brands vary in heat, so you may want to add more or less, depending on which you purchase and your taste. You can substitute Aleppo pepper or, in a pinch, cayenne (also hot, but less interesting than harissa and Aleppo).

Makes 1 tart for 4 servings

¾ pound carrots, peeled

2 tablespoons extra-virgin olive oil

½ cup thinly sliced onion

1 garlic clove, thinly sliced

1½ cups small shreds roast chicken

Fine sea salt

4 teaspoons harissa, or to taste

½ teaspoon ground cumin

3 tablespoons heavy cream

1 teaspoon fresh lemon juice

1 large egg yolk

1 sheet frozen puff pastry (half of 17-ounce package), thawed

6 dry-cured pitted black olives, quartered lengthwise

1¼ teaspoons cumin seeds

3 tablespoons crumbled feta cheese (about 1½ ounces)

1½ tablespoons finely chopped fresh cilantro or parsley leaves

Bring a large pot of salted water to a boil. Add the carrots, partially cover, and cook until just tender, 12 to 15 minutes, depending on the size.

Meanwhile, in a 12-inch skillet, heat the oil over medium-high heat. Add the onion and garlic, reduce the heat to medium-low, and cook, stirring occasionally, until softened but not browned, about 7 minutes. Using tongs or a slotted spoon, transfer to a large bowl. Reserve the skillet.

Drain the carrots and run under cold water to cool, then slice on a long diagonal into 1/16-inch-thick slices. Put half of the slices (about ¾ cup) into the bowl with the onions, and the other half into the reserved skillet.

To the carrot-onion mixture, add the chicken and ¼ teaspoon salt; gently stir to combine. Add harissa.

Sprinkle the cumin and ½ teaspoon salt over the carrots in the skillet, then heat over medium-high heat, stirring occasionally to evenly distribute the spices, for 1 minute. Transfer to the bowl of a food processor or a blender, add 2 tablespoons of the cream and the lemon juice, and purée until smooth.

Preheat the oven to 400°F with the rack in the lower third of the oven.

Whisk together the remaining 1 tablespoon cream and the egg yolk. On a sheet of parchment paper, roll out the puff pastry to a 10x12-inch rectangle. Brush with the egg wash, then crimp the edges to form a ¼- to ⅓-inch border. Prick all over with a fork. Slide with the parchment paper onto a baking sheet and freeze for 15 minutes.

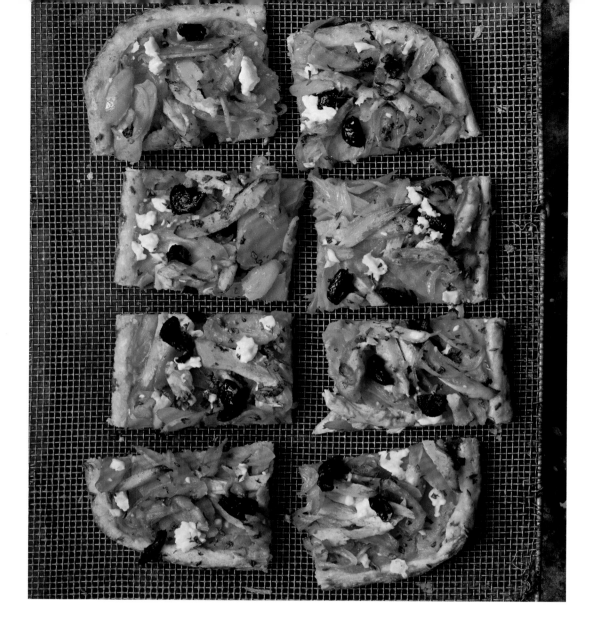

Spread the pastry with the carrot purée in an even layer, then freeze for 15 minutes more. Arrange the carrot-chicken mixture over the purée and sprinkle with the olives. Sprinkle the edges of the pastry with the cumin seeds.

Bake until the edges are golden and puffed, 20 to 25 minutes, then sprinkle with the cheese and bake for 5 minutes more.

Let the tart cool on a wire rack. Serve warm or at room temperature, sprinkling with the cilantro just before serving.

ROAST CHICKEN in LAVASH with TOASTED FENNEL, CORIANDER, and CUMIN YOGURT

Serves 4

Basic pantry spices, freshly toasted and ground, send a wonderful fragrance wafting through the house and turn Greek yogurt into a bright, creamy dressing for this healthful sandwich. Lavash is a thin, soft Middle Eastern flatbread, similar to a whole-wheat tortilla. Look for it in specialty food stores, health food stores, and good supermarkets.

1 teaspoon fennel seeds

1 teaspoon coriander seeds

½ teaspoon cumin seeds

¾ cup Greek yogurt

2½ tablespoons finely chopped fresh chives

1½ tablespoons fresh lemon juice

Fine sea salt

Freshly ground black pepper

2 cups medium shreds roast chicken, at room temperature

1 large cucumber, peeled and cut into ⅛-inch slices on a long diagonal

4 radishes, thinly sliced

1 tablespoon extra-virgin olive oil

2 (16-to 20-inch-round) very thin pliable lavash, or 4 (8-inch) flour tortillas or wraps

1 cup loosely packed fresh cilantro leaves

Combine the fennel, coriander, and cumin seeds in a small skillet. Heat over low heat, occasionally shaking the pan back and forth until the seeds are fragrant and lightly toasted, about 3 minutes. Transfer the spices to a plate and let cool for a few minutes, then finely grind in a spice grinder or mortar and pestle.

In a medium bowl, whisk together the spice mixture, yogurt, chives, lemon juice, 1 teaspoon salt, and a generous pinch of pepper. Add the chicken and stir to coat with the yogurt sauce.

In a second bowl, toss together the cucumber, radishes, oil, and a generous pinch of salt and pepper.

Cut the lavash into four 8x8-inch squares. Place the squares on a clean work surface. Spread the chicken mixture on the ends nearest you, leaving a 1-inch border on each side. Top with the cucumber-radish mixture and the cilantro. Fold up the bottom, left side, and right side of the lavash before rolling away from you. If using tortillas or wraps, fill and roll up in the same manner.

ROAST CHICKEN *with* RAJAS (POBLANO CHILES *and* CREAM)

Serves 4

Creamy, spicy, and rich, this delicious Mexican dish is made with crème fraîche, a tangy thickened cream found in the supermarket's dairy section (sour cream doesn't work as a substitute; you'll wind up with a soupy sauce). If you plan ahead, you can make your own crème fraîche (see Box). Serve this dish with rice, tortillas, or both.

2½ pounds poblano chiles

3 tablespoons extra-virgin olive oil

2 cups thinly sliced Vidalia or other sweet onions

½ teaspoon fine sea salt

2 cups crème fraîche

⅓ cup whole milk

⅛ teaspoon ground cumin

3 cups medium shreds roast chicken

½ cup coarsely chopped cilantro, optional

making crème fraîche

To make 2 cups of crème fraîche, combine 2 cups heavy cream (pasteurized, not ultra-pasteurized or sterilized, and without additives), and 2 tablespoons cultured buttermilk in a medium saucepan. Over low heat, bring the mixture to tepid temperature (not more than 85ºF on an instant-read thermometer). Transfer to a clean glass container. Partially cover and let stand at warm room temperature (70º to 75ºF) for 8 to 24 hours, or until very thick. Stir well, cover, and refrigerate for 24 hours before using, or up to 10 days.

Char the chiles directly over gas burners set on high, on a grill pan over high heat, or on a hot grill, turning frequently, until blackened and blistered on all sides. Transfer to a large bowl and cover tightly with plastic wrap; let sit for 10 minutes.

Preheat the oven to 375ºF with the rack in the middle.

If your skin is sensitive when working with chiles, put on rubber gloves before using your fingers to rub off the chile skins. Dip your hands into a bowl of water to rinse off the pepper skin bits as you go (do not rinse the peppers, otherwise you'll rinse away a good deal of their flavor along with the skins), then seed the peppers and slice lengthwise into ⅛-inch strips. Cut the strips in half crosswise.

Heat the oil in a 12-inch skillet over medium-high heat. Add the onions, reduce the heat to medium, and cook, stirring frequently, until softened, about 8 minutes. Stir in all but 1 cup of the chile strips. Cover and cook 5 minutes more, then stir in salt and remove the skillet from the heat.

In a blender, combine the reserved cup of chile strips, crème fraîche, milk, and cumin; purée until smooth. If necessary, turn the blender off and use a rubber spatula to stir the mixture and help incorporate the milk. Then continue to purée.

In a 2-quart baking dish, layer half of the chicken, half of the onion mixture, and half of the sauce. Repeat to make a second layer with the remaining ingredients. Bake until hot, 25 to 30 minutes. Serve warm, sprinkled with cilantro, if desired.

3 PITZAS (2 GREEK and A LEBANESE)

These Mediterranean "pitzas" make good cocktail snacks, dinner party appetizers, or a nice meal on their own. I recommend using a pizza stone; they are inexpensive, easy to use, and produce a crispy crust. A pizza peel is great for rolling out the dough on, and, with a little practice, you'll be using it to slide pies right onto the stone.

GREEK PITZA

Leeks, Swiss chard, and currants may not be what you think of when it comes to Greek cuisine, but, in fact, they are very typical ingredients and make a lovely pie.

Makes 4 8-inch Greek pitzas

DOUGH

3 cups unbleached all-purpose flour

1 teaspoon fine sea salt

1 (¼-ounce) package active dry yeast (2¼ teaspoons)

½ teaspoon sugar

¼ cup extra-virgin olive oil

TOPPING

1 tablespoon unsalted butter

5½ tablespoons extra-virgin olive oil

2 leeks, white and light green parts only, thinly sliced, thoroughly washed and patted dry

Flaky coarse sea salt

3 pounds red Swiss chard (about 2 large bunches)

4 garlic cloves

2 tablespoons plus 2 teaspoons currants

To make the dough: Whisk together the flour and fine salt in a large bowl. Put the yeast in a small bowl, add 1 cup warm water (about 105°F), then the sugar. Stir just to combine and let stand until foamy, about 5 minutes. (If the mixture doesn't foam, discard and start over with new yeast.) Make a small well in the flour mixture and add the oil; stir to combine, then add the yeast mixture and, using your hands, mix to form a dough. Transfer the dough to a lightly floured work surface and knead for 5 minutes, then put the dough in a lightly oiled bowl, cover the bowl with a clean dish towel, and let sit in a draft-free warm room for 1½ hours.

Preheat the oven to 500°F with the rack in the middle and a pizza stone on the rack.

Heat the butter and ½ tablespoon oil in a small skillet over medium heat until the butter is melted. Add the leeks and a pinch of coarse salt, reduce the heat to low and cook, stirring occasionally, until softened and sweet, about 20 minutes.

Meanwhile, cut the stems and center ribs from the chard, discarding any tough portions, then cut the stems and ribs crosswise into 1-inch pieces. Roughly chop the chard leaves.

Wash the chard and partially spin-dry, leaving some moisture on the leaves for cooking. Heat 1 tablespoon oil in a 5- to 6-quart Dutch oven or other heavy pot over medium heat, then add the chard. Cover and

Heaping 1 cup small to medium shreds roast chicken

½ cup crumbled feta cheese (about 2½ ounces)

Fresh minced hot chile or red pepper flakes

cook for 1 minute, then stir. Continue to cook, covered, stirring every minute or so, until wilted and tender, 3 to 4 minutes total. Drain the chard in a colander and let sit until cool enough to handle, then squeeze all of the excess liquid from the chard, finely chop, and put into a bowl.

Form ¼ of the dough into a ball, then shape the ball into a disc. On a lightly floured pizza peel, roll out the dough into an 8- to 9-inch round. Leaving a 1-inch border, spread 1 tablespoon oil on the dough. Thinly slice 1 garlic clove and sprinkle on top of the oil, then top with 2 teaspoons currants, then a quarter of the chard and a quarter of the chicken.

Slide the pitza onto the stone and bake until the edges and bottom of the crust are golden, 6 to 8 minutes. Use the peel to remove the pitza from the oven and transfer to a cutting board. Immediately top with a quarter of the leeks and cheese, sprinkle with the chile, and cut into pieces. Repeat to make three more pitzas.

GREEK PITZA VARIATION

Dried Greek oregano, often sold on its branches in cellophane bags, rather than crumbled into jars, is worlds more fragrant and flavorful than the average supermarket counterpart. I use it for all of my oregano needs. See Sources and Credits, page 170, for shopping suggestions.

Makes 4 8-inch Greek pitzas

1 batch dough (page 161)

TOPPING

4 tablespoons extra-virgin olive oil

4 garlic cloves

4 small tomatoes (1 pound total), thinly sliced crosswise

2 small red onions, very thinly sliced

2 teaspoons dried oregano, preferably Greek

Flaky coarse sea salt

Heaping 1 cup small shreds roast chicken

2 teaspoons fresh lemon juice (optional)

Repeat the instructions on page 161 and above for making the dough, preheating the oven and pizza stone (heating the stone for at least 20 minutes before baking pitzas), dividing the dough, and rolling out the dough on a lightly floured peel.

Leaving a 1-inch border, spread 1 tablespoon oil on the dough. Thinly slice 1 garlic clove and sprinkle on top of the oil, then top with a quarter of the tomatoes, a quarter of the onions, a sprinkle each of oregano and salt, a quarter of the chicken, and a few drops of lemon juice.

Slide the pitza onto the stone and bake until the edges and bottom of the crust are golden, 6 to 8 minutes. Use the peel to remove the pitza from the oven and transfer to a cutting board. Cut into pieces. Repeat to make three more pitzas.

LEBANESE PITZA

This is a less labor-intensive affair than either of the two Greek pitzas, yet just as good.

1 batch dough (page 161)

TOPPING

4 tablespoons extra-virgin olive oil

4 garlic cloves

4 teaspoons za'atar

2 small red onions

1⅓ cups small to medium shreds roast chicken

Flaky coarse sea salt

Repeat the instructions on pages 161 and 162 for making the dough, preheating the oven and pizza stone (heating the stone for at least 20 minutes before baking pitzas), dividing the dough, and rolling out the dough on a lightly floured peel.

Leaving a 1-inch border, spread 1 tablespoon oil on the dough. Thinly slice 1 garlic clove and sprinkle on top of the oil, then top with ½ teaspoon za'atar, a quarter of the onions, a quarter of the chicken, an additional ½ teaspoon za'atar, and a sprinkle of salt.

Slide the pitza onto the stone and bake until the edges and bottom of the crust are golden, 6 to 8 minutes. Use the peel to remove the pitza from the oven and transfer to a cutting board. Cut into pieces. Repeat to make three more pitzas.

ROAST CHICKEN POT PIE
with WINTER VEGETABLES

Most pot pies are prepared with the puff pastry draped over the pie filling, then baked to heat the creamy sauce, meat, vegetables, and puff pastry in one go. It looks pretty, but the pastry is often damp and soggy in spots since—when laid over the wet filling, then baked—it doesn't have a chance to dry out fully and rise. Here, the pastry is cut and baked separately, which allows it to reach its fullest golden flakiness, then it is stacked with the piping-hot filling to serve. If you're not serving six people, you can defrost and bake only the pastry you need; extra filling can be kept, chilled, in an airtight container for up to 3 days, or frozen for up to 1 month.

12 small to medium cipollini or pearl onions

2½ tablespoons unsalted butter

3 cups chicken broth, preferably homemade (page 100)

4 cups (⅓-inch cubes) mixed root vegetables, such as parsnips, carrots, butternut squash, rutabaga, sweet potato, and/or celery root

2 ounces thick cut bacon (about 2 slices), cut crosswise into 1-inch pieces

2 garlic cloves, thinly sliced

1 tablespoon finely chopped fresh rosemary leaves

2 tablespoons unbleached all-purpose flour

⅔ cup plus 2 tablespoons crème fraîche

2 cups medium shreds skinless roast chicken

½ teaspoon fine sea salt

Freshly ground black pepper

Preheat the oven to 400°F with the racks positioned in the middle and lower third of the oven. Line a baking sheet with parchment paper.

Blanch the onions in a pot of boiling water for 1 minute and drain, then cool under running water. Trim the root ends and peel.

In a heavy saucepan, melt 1 tablespoon butter over medium heat. Add the onions, reduce heat to low, and cook, stirring occasionally, until lightly golden, about 3 minutes. Add the broth, bring to a simmer, and cook, partially covered, for 7 minutes. Add the root vegetables and continue to simmer, partially covered, until the vegetables are just tender, about 8 minutes more. Over a bowl, strain the vegetables; reserve the broth. Put the vegetables into a large bowl.

In a medium nonstick skillet, cook the bacon over medium heat until lightly golden, about 5 minutes, then stir in the garlic and rosemary and cook for 1 minute more. Using a slotted spoon, transfer to the bowl with the vegetables; reserve the skillet.

Add the remaining 1½ tablespoons butter to the skillet; heat over medium heat until the butter is melted, then stir in the flour. Reduce the heat to low and cook the flour, stirring constantly, for 3 minutes. Remove the skillet from the heat, add the crème fraîche and stir to combine. Stir the crème fraîche mixture into the vegetable mixture. Add the chicken, ½ cup of the reserved broth, the fine salt, and ¼ teaspoon pepper; stir to combine well, then transfer to a 2-quart baking dish. Cover tightly with foil.

1 sheet frozen puff pastry (half of 17-ounce package), thawed

1 large egg yolk, lightly beaten with a touch of water

Flaky coarse sea salt

Unfold the pastry onto a clean, lightly floured work surface. Cut into 12 (2¼ x3–inch) rectangles and transfer to the prepared baking sheet. Brush the tops with the egg wash; sprinkle with coarse salt and pepper. Put the puff pastry on the lower rack and the filling on the middle rack.

Bake, rotating the puff pastry once halfway through, until puffed and golden, about 15 minutes.

Put one pastry rectangle in each serving bowl; top with the filling and a second pastry rectangle. Serve warm.

TORTILLA ESPAÑOLA *with* CHORIZO *and* SHREDDED ROAST CHICKEN

Tortilla Española—comprised of thin potato slices gently simmered in a hot bath of extra-virgin olive oil, then cooked with onion and egg into a thick omelette—is among the most beloved and ubiquitous of Spanish tapas. Eaten at room temperature, a tortilla makes for great cocktail, snack, or picnic fare, cut into wedges or small squares. A slice on a baguette is also a delicious sandwich. Chorizo and shreds of roast chicken, though uncommon, are tasty additions. A hand held mandoline slicer makes cutting potatoes into thin slices easy, but a good sharp chef's knife will do the trick, too.

Serves 4 as a main course; 8 as tapas

¾ cup olive oil

1 pound Yukon gold potatoes, cut crosswise into ¹⁄₁₆-inch slices

1 medium yellow onion, finely chopped

Fine sea salt

1½ ounces fully cooked Mexican or Spanish chorizo, cut into small cubes (about ½ cup)

6 large eggs

1 cup medium shreds roast chicken

Freshly ground black pepper

In a 9- to 10-inch skillet, heat the oil over medium heat until hot but not smoking. Add the potatoes and onion. Sprinkle with ½ teaspoon salt, reduce the heat to medium-low, and cook, gently stirring, turning and pressing the mixture occasionally to keep it submerged in the oil, for 20 minutes. Gently stir in the chorizo and continue to cook for 20 minutes more.

Drain the mixture in a colander set over a clean dry bowl (reserve the oil and the skillet). Meanwhile, in a large bowl, lightly beat the eggs.

Beat in 1 tablespoon of the reserved oil to the eggs, then add the potato mixture and chicken and gently stir to combine. Add ½ teaspoon salt and generous pepper; gently stir once more.

Add 1 tablespoon of the reserved oil to the skillet and heat over low heat. Add the potato mixture, spreading the mixture into the pan in an even layer and pressing gently. Cook, covered, until the eggs are almost set, 12 to 15 minutes. Turn off the heat and let the skillet sit, covered, for 15 minutes.

Uncover the skillet and, in one quick but careful motion, invert the tortilla onto a large plate. Slide the tortilla back into the skillet. Cook over low heat, covered, until the eggs are set, about 5 minutes more (the center will still be juicy; take care not to overcook the eggs).

Slide the tortilla back onto the plate and let cool to warm or room temperature. Cut into slices or cubes.

ROAST CHICKEN *and* FRESH HERB SUMMER ROLLS

Like many Vietnamese dishes, these summer rolls, filled with fresh herbs, cucumber, and roast chicken, have a refreshingly clean taste. If you're new to the technique, don't fret: Once you get a feel for working with the rice-paper rounds, the rolls are fun and easy to make.

Serves 4

Good basic kitchen salt, like kosher (for water)

1 teaspoon fine sea salt

½ teaspoon ground coriander

½ cup thinly sliced skinless roast chicken

2 teaspoons hoisin sauce (see Sources and Credits, page 170)

1 ounce bean thread noodles

1 tablespoon rice vinegar

1 tablespoon plus 1 teaspoon sugar

1 medium cucumber

4 (8-inch) rice-paper rounds, plus extra in case some tear

¼ cup fresh mint leaves

¼ cup fresh basil leaves, preferably Thai

4 small or 2 large shiitake mushrooms, stems trimmed and caps thinly sliced

1 medium carrot, coarsely shredded

4 teaspoons finely chopped roasted and salted peanuts

Sriracha sauce for dipping (see Sources and Credits, page 170)

Bring a medium saucepan of well-salted water to a boil. Meanwhile, in a small bowl, mix together ½ teaspoon fine salt and the coriander. In a second small bowl, mix together the chicken and hoisin sauce.

Add the noodles to the boiling water and cook until just tender, about 3 minutes. Drain in a colander, then rinse under cold running water and drain well. Stir together the vinegar, sugar, and remaining ½ teaspoon fine salt in a large bowl until the sugar is dissolved, then add the noodles and toss to coat.

Peel and seed the cucumber, then cut in half or into thirds. Cut each portion into ⅛-inch-thick matchsticks.

Fill a shallow baking pan with warm water. Check the rice-paper rounds and use only those that have no holes. Soak 1 round in warm water until pliable, 30 seconds to 1 minute, then carefully transfer to a clean work surface. Blot dry with paper towels.

Arrange a quarter of the chicken mixture in a row across the bottom third of the soaked rice paper. Spread ¼ cup noodles on top of the chicken and arrange a quarter of the mint leaves, a quarter of the basil leaves, a quarter of the cucumber matchsticks, a quarter of the mushrooms, a quarter of the carrot, and a quarter of the peanuts, horizontally on top of noodles. Sprinkle with the salt mixture.

Fold the bottom of the rice paper over the filling and begin rolling up tightly, stopping at the halfway point, then fold in the ends and continue rolling. Put the summer roll, seam-side down, on a plate and cover with dampened paper towels. Make three more rolls in the same manner and serve, whole or halved diagonally, with Sriracha sauce for dipping.

CHINESE ROAST CHICKEN BUNS *with* SCALLION *and* SPICY HOISIN SAUCE

Serves 4

Tender meat—often pork, though here, it's chicken—sweet, garlicky hoisin sauce, cooling cucumber, and scallion all tucked into soft pillowy steamed dough; no wonder everyone seems crazy for Chinese buns these days. The Tea-Brined Five-Spice Roast Chicken, page 41, is delicious here. Packaged buns can be purchased at Asian markets if you don't have time to make and steam your own dough.

1 cup unbleached all-purpose flour

½ cup cake flour

1½ teaspoons active dry yeast

1½ teaspoons sugar

⅛ teaspoon fine sea salt

1 teaspoon vegetable oil, plus more for brushing dough

1 pound sliced roast chicken, preferably Tea-Brined Five-Spice Roast Chicken (page 41), preferably with skin (3½–4 cups)

Hoisin sauce (see Sources and Credits, page 170)

Sriracha sauce (see Sources and Credits, page 170)

1 medium cucumber, thinly sliced crosswise

5 to 6 scallions, trimmed and julienned or thinly sliced on a long diagonal

Special equipment: A pasta pot with a deep perforated colander-steamer insert or a bamboo or metal steamer

In a large bowl, whisk together the flour, cake flour, yeast, sugar, and salt; add ½ cup warm water (around 105°F) and oil. Using your hands, mix and then knead in the bowl until a dough forms (add up to ¼ cup more water by the tablespoonful, if necessary). Turn out the dough onto a lightly floured work surface and knead until smooth and elastic, about 5 minutes. Put the dough into an oiled bowl, turning the dough to coat it with oil, then cover with a clean dish towel and let rise in a draft-free warm room until doubled in size, 45 minutes to 1 hour. Meanwhile, cut out 12 (2½x2½-inch) squares of parchment paper.

Punch down the dough and form it into a 1¾-inch-thick rope. Cut into 12 equal pieces. Roll each piece into a ball. Place balls on a baking sheet, cover loosely with plastic wrap, and let rise at a warm room temperature for 30 minutes.

Pat each ball into a long oval, about 5x2 inches, ⅛ inch thick. Brush 1 oval with oil, then fold in half crosswise, place on a parchment square, and brush with oil again. Place on a baking sheet and repeat with the remaining dough pieces. Loosely cover the buns with plastic wrap and let rise at a warm room temperature until nearly doubled in size, about 30 minutes.

Add enough water to a pot so that the bottom of a steamer insert sits above the water. Bring to a simmer. Arrange the buns, in batches, if necessary, about ½ inch apart, on the insert and steam over medium heat, covered, until the dough is slightly puffed and cooked through, about 10 minutes.

Layer each bun with chicken, hoisin, Sriracha, cucumber, and scallions.

SOURCES AND CREDITS

ASIAN PRODUCTS

Chile-garlic sauce, Sriracha sauce, fish sauce, hoisin sauce, sheets of nori, kimchi, lemongrass, fresh ginger, galangal, and sushi rice can be found in the Asian sections at most good supermarkets (kimchi will be in the refrigerated section; lemongrass, fresh ginger, and galangal will be in produce). *Kochujang* (Korean chili-soybean paste) and products above can be found at Korean markets.

CAPERS

Salt-packed capers are available at specialty shops, and at www.gustiamo.com and Buon Italia (75 9th Avenue, New York, NY 10011; 212-633-9090; www.buonitalia.com).

CHICKEN

"Good birds" can be found at local farmers' markets, good butcher shops, and good supermarkets, such as Whole Foods Market, www.wholefoods.com. Regional and national brands, like Murray's Chicken, www.murrayschicken.com, and Eberly, www.eberlypoultry.com, offer antibiotic- and hormone-free, and organic birds. For a state-by-state directory of grass-fed poultry and meat, and for information about, and sources for, heritage breeds, see www.eatwild.com, www.localharvest.org, and www.sustainabletable.org..

CHORIZO AND MORCILLA SAUSAGES

Despaña (408 Broome Street, New York, NY 10013; 212-219-5050; www.despananyc.com) is my go-to source for chorizo and morcilla sausages, as well as Spanish olive oils, vinegars, and other fine products from Spain.

DRIED BEANS, GRAINS, AND LEGUMES

For colfiorito lentils, go to www.gustiamo. com. Look for French green lentils at fine supermarkets, like Whole Foods Market, www.wholefoodsmarket.com. Spanish pardina lentils can be ordered from Despaña (408 Broome Street, New York, NY 10013; 212-219-5050; www.despananyc.com).

At Rancho Gordo, www.ranchogordo.com, you can purchase fantastic dried heirloom beans by mail order. Giganti beans can be mail-ordered from Titan Foods (2556 31st Street, Long Island City, NY 11102; 718-626-7771; www.titanfood.com). Good-quality dried beans can also be purchased from a reputable grocer or specialty shop and used by "best by" date.

Farro can be purchased at Whole Foods Market, www.wholefoodsmarket.com; Buon Italia (75 9th Avenue, New York, NY 10011; 212-633-9090; www.buonitalia.com); and Rubiner's Cheesemongers & Grocers (264 Main Street, Great Barrington, MA 01230; 413-528-0488), which also stocks a fantastic selection of cheeses, olive oils, cured meats, spices, and more.

The finest freekeh I know is from Cayuga Pure Organics (607-229-6429; www. cporganics.com).

For an extensive selection of dried beans, grains, and legumes, visit Kalustyan's (123 Lexington Avenue, New York, NY 10016; 212-685-3451; www.kalustyans.com).

DRIED CHILES

Look for whole dried chiles at Mexican markets, or order from Amazon (www. amazon.com).

HARISSA

My favorite brands of harissa, m'hamsa, and spicy sun-dried tomato spread are made by a company called Les Moulins Mahjoub, which is distributed in the US by the Rogers Collection. Look for the brand at Whole Foods Market, www.wholefoodsmarket.com, and Le Pain Quotidien, www.painquotidien. com, or see www.therogerscollection.com or call (207) 828-2000, for information on stores in your area that stock the products. The Rogers Collection is also a terrific resource for fine olive oils.

HERBS

Dried Greek oregano and other high-quality dried herbs can be purchased at Buon Italia (75 9th Avenue, New York, NY 10011; 212-633-9090; www.buonitalia.com) and Titan Foods (2556 31st Street, Long Island City, NY 11102-1722; 718-626-7771; www.titanfood.com).

M'HAMSA

See Harissa

NUTS

Purchase Marcona almonds at Whole Foods Market, www.wholefoodsmarket.com; or Despaña (408 Broome Street, New York, NY 10013; 212-219-5050; www.despananyc.com).

OLIVES AND OLIVE OILS

Look for Lucques and Cerignola olives at specialty food shops, or order them from Formaggio Kitchen (244 Huron Avenue, Cambridge, MA 02138; 888-212-3224; www.formaggiokitchen.com).

For a terrific selection of estate-bottled extra-virgin olive oils from Italy, look to www. gustiamo.com. Fantastic Spanish olives and olive oils, including Castillo de Canena, and other fine products from Spain, can be found at Despaña (408 Broome Street, New York, NY 10013; 212-219-5050; www.despananyc.com). Look for a great selection of fine estate-bottled extra-virgin olive oils at Rubiner's Cheesemongers & Grocers (264 Main Street, Great Barrington, MA 01230; 413-528-0488).

PASTA

My favorite dried pasta is Pasta Setaro. An extensive line of the product, as well as high-quality farro and whole-wheat pastas can be found at Buon Italia (75 9th Avenue, New York, NY 10011; 212-633-9090; www.buonitalia.com).

POTS, PANS, AND TOOLS

I rely heavily on Le Creuset (www.lecreuset.

co.uk/en-us/) enameled cast-iron gratin dishes, grill pans, and Dutch ovens, for cooking chicken and more.

Berndes makes fantastic nonstick skillets. I recommend the "Tradition" line, which is made using vacuum-pressured casting. These pans heat well and evenly; the coating does not chip or peel. With wooden handles wrapped in foil, the pans can be used in the oven. Look for them on Amazon (www.amazon.com).

Shop Lodge (www.lodgemfg.com) for cast-iron skillets.

Joyce Chen Scissors are invaluable for cutting the backbone out of a chicken, snipping herbs, and more. Look for them on Amazon (www.amazon.com).

RICE
Sushi rice can be purchased at good supermarkets, Asian markets, and Amazon(www.amazon.com).

Bomba and Calasparra rices can be purchased at Despaña (408 Broome Street, New York, NY 10013; 212-219-5050; www.despananyc.com).

SEA SALT
Fantastic fine and flaky coarse sea salts can be purchased at Rubiner's Cheesemongers & Grocers (264 Main Street, Great Barrington, MA 01230;413-528-0488), and The Meadow (3731 N. Mississippi Avenue, Portland, OR 97227; 888-388-4633). Among my favorite salts are Big Tree Farms Coarse Hollow Pyramids and Fine Grain (Fleur de Sel); both can be purchased from Amazon (www.amazon.com).

SPICES
Wild fennel pollen, Aleppo pepper, and other high-quality spices and food products can be purchased at Zingerman's (620 Phoenix Drive, Ann Arbor, Michigan 48108; 888-636-8162; www.zingermans.com) and Rubiner's

Cheesemongers & Grocers (264 Main Street, Great Barrington, MA 01230; 413-528-0488)

Kalustyan's (123 Lexington Avenue, New York, NY 10016; 212-685-3451; www. kalustyans.com) stocks a fine selection of high-quality spices, including berbere spice, sumac, and za'atar, as well as wonderfully aromatic black peppercorns.

For Pimentón de la Vera, contact Despaña (408 Broome Street, New York, NY 10013; 212-219-5050; www.despananyc.com).

SUN-DRIED TOMATO SPREAD
See Harissa

Beautiful things and good kitchenware that appear in this book

Ochre (462 Broome Street, New York, NY 10013; 212-414-4332; www.ochrestore.com)
Page 42: Linen surface
Page 80: Bowl
Page 124: Bowls
Page 136: All dishes, except empty bowl
Page 168: Small bowl

Le Crueset (www.lecreuset.co.uk/en-us/)
Page 26: Oval French Oven, 5-quart
Page 35: Oval Au Gratin, 3-quart
Page 98: Stockpot, 8-quart

INDEX